YOUR
MINISTRY OF
EVANGELISM

A GUIDE FOR
CHURCH VOLUNTEERS

by

Elmer L. Towns, Th.M., D.D.

EVANGELICAL TRAINING ASSOCIATION
110 Bridge Street • Box 327
Wheaton, Illinois 60189

This text replaces *Evangelize Thru Christian Education*.

Scripture quotations are from the King James Version Bible unless otherwise noted. Other quotations are from the New International Version (NIV), © 1973, The New York Bible Society International.

2004 Edition

ISBN: 0-910566-48-8

CONTENTS

INTRODUCTION

Evangelism is the mandate for church growth today. Numerical as well as spiritual growth result from evangelism in church ministry. Without evangelism the church program becomes routine and unproductive.

After self-evaluation, few Christians can be proud of their evangelistic efforts. Although all believers may not have the gift of evangelism, all should be able to witness to their faith in Christ and have a part in the church's evangelistic effort. When all church members can do this, all who come into contact with the church will be confronted with the gospel message and face a decision concerning their relationship to Christ.

Knowing the content of the Bible simply provides the basis of evangelism. Knowing Christian ethics merely provides guidelines for proper conduct. Neither a knowledge of the Word without acceptance of its message nor an ethical life without Christ is Christianity. As a Christian, your ministry of evangelism enables you to relate knowledge to life and open the way to eternal salvation to all with whom you come in contact. It is evangelism which gives balance to your ministry and makes you effective in serving Christ.

The format of this book is simple to follow. The content is well outlined to help you to remember and refer back to the important points covered in each chapter. Footnotes are numbered and appear at the end of each chapter. Also, at the conclusion of each chapter you will find content review and discussion questions as well as application activities. A bibliography of current texts is found at the end of the book.

This book is helpful reading for all church volunteers whether or not it is studied as a part of class requirements.

CULTURAL MANDATE
FOR
EVANGELISM

$$\boxed{1}$$

Jesus' last command to "make disciples" (Matt. 28:19) should be the first concern of every church ministry and individual Christian. The Lord loved the unsaved so much that He provided the means for their salvation (John 3:16), urged His disciples to pray for laborers for the harvest (Matt. 9:38), and empowered and appointed His disciples as witnesses (Acts 1:8). Although the message of the gospel has not changed, there are different strategies in every generation which prove effective in reaching the lost for Christ. Rather than holding to traditional methods because "that's the way it has always been done," Christians should be seeking to examine new approaches and incorporate them into their evangelism strategy.

Three kinds of evangelism

Dr. Peter Wagner, well-known church growth consultant, has identified three types of evangelism. He terms these *presence evangelism, proclamation evangelism,* and *persuasion evangelism.*

Presence evangelism

Presence evangelism stems from the biblical word for "witness" or "testimony." Christians evangelize by living God-honoring lives before the lost. Hopefully as non-believers witness Christians who are living distinct lifestyles, they will want to know more about the gospel and ultimately come to Christ. This involves giving testimony of what Christ has done in your life, or sharing your faith with others. Sometimes this is also called *lifestyle evangelism.*

On the mission field, *presence evangelism* may take the form of medical evangelism or agricultural evangelism. In some Moslem countries where missionaries are prohibited from entering, Christian businessmen evangelize by their presence. When people reflect the attitudes or character of Jesus Christ, they are witnessing the gospel. Also included in *presence evangelism* is what is usually called charity or social action, i.e. "giving a cup of cold water" in the name of Christ.

Proclamation evangelism

In *proclamation evangelism*, Christians make the good news of Jesus Christ clearly known so that the lost will understand. John R. Mott defined evangelism as "the declaration of the gospel of Christ either privately or publicly, by a messenger of God so that men might repent of their sin, turn to God, and live abundantly."[1] This view differs slightly from the historic definition of evangelism as represented by a 1918 statement by a group of Anglican archbishops which claimed, "To evangelize is so to present Christ Jesus in the power of the Holy Spirit, that men and women shall come to put their trust in God through Him, to accept Him as their Saviour, and serve Him as their King in the fellowship of His Church."[2] According to Mott, a positive response to the gospel may be desirable, but is not necessarily an integral part of evangelism. *Proclamation evangelism* is simply proclaiming the gospel in the power of the Holy Spirit and leaving the results to God. *leaving the results to God.*

Persuasion evangelism *Sunday School, one on one*

Persuasion evangelism involves not only proclaiming the gospel, but also persuading or motivating the unsaved to respond. If the process of proclaiming the gospel is effective, the evangelist should compel the lost to come to Christ. *Persuasion evangelism* is intentionally preaching so that there are results, such as believers being added to the church.

Those who believe in *persuasion evangelism* claim that the command, "Go therefore and make disciples" (Matt. 28:19) implies the minister has an obligation to seek results in evangelism. Disciples are the result of evangelism.

Evangelism in three stages

Perhaps the best way to understand the relationship between the three kinds of evangelism described above is to understand the three stages which are involved in the evangelism process. First, Christians begin with presence evangelism in order to "win a hearing." They must have good testimonies and be interested in the needs of the lost. The godly lives of Christians will hopefully motivate the lost to give an honest hearing to the gospel.

Next, they must proclaim the gospel to the unsaved. Before people can be saved, they must hear the gospel and understand its message. Witnessing Christians must not add works to the gospel, nor must they dilute its obligations.

Finally, evangelists must persuade people to receive Christ. At times Paul pleaded with tears (Rom. 9:2; 10:1), while at other times he persuaded as a trial lawyer often does (Acts 13:43).

Nine words to describe evangelism

In studying the evangelistic activity of the early church, it is apparent that different circumstances and conditions required different approaches to evangelism. At least nine words are used in the New Testament to describe the evangelism that took place in the early church. Examining these words can give Christians today insight into various ways they can share their own faith.

Martureō - Sharing your experience with others

First, Christians are to witness. Jesus said, "You shall be my witnesses" (Acts 1:8). Witnesses share what they have seen and heard. This Greek verb *martureō* is related to the English word "martyr" and implies both being and bearing a witness.

Laleō - Talking to others

A second Greek verb used to describe New Testament evangelism is *laleō* which means to talk or use the voice. The expression "as they spake to the people" (Acts 4:1) simply means they communicated a message. The emphasis is not so much on what they communicated, but rather that they were sharing the gospel as they spoke to the people.

Euaggelizō - Telling others about Jesus

Third, the New Testament Christians evangelized, or told others the good news about Jesus. "Therefore they that were scattered abroad went everywhere preaching (evangelizing) the word" (Acts 8:4). The word *evangelize* means "to gospelize," or "to give the gospel message." Evangelizing means to announce a good news message. Implied in this term is an emphasis on the message or matter announced.

Didaskō - Teaching others the gospel systematically

A fourth kind of New Testament evangelism involves the systematic teaching of the gospel. Jesus spoke of "teaching them to observe all things that I have commanded you" (Matt. 28:20). The Greek word *didaskō* suggests a systematic explanation of the gospel so people can understand and believe.

Dialēgomai - Answering reasonable objections

When Paul and others in the New Testament engaged in evangelism, they often had to answer reasonable objections which were raised to the gospel message. The Greek word *dialēgomai* means "to reason" or "to respond to objections" and suggests that Paul's evangelism at times resembled a question and answer session. "And he reasoned in the synagogue" (Acts 18:4).

Kataggĕllō - Driving home the gospel
A sixth word used to describe evangelism is *kataggĕllō*, which implies the "driving home" of an idea. Effective evangelism reaches people at their point of need. When the unsaved realize how Jesus can meet that need in their life, they can be led to conclude "Jesus, whom I preach unto you, is Christ" (Acts 17:3).

Kērussō - Announcing the gospel so people can respond
The early church proclaimed, or *kērussō*, the gospel so that people could understand it. They "preached Christ to them" (Acts 8:5). This Greek verb is sometimes translated "heralding." It refers to proclaiming as a herald and does not necessarily make reference to a decision or a gospel invitation.

Mathateuō - Convincing others to follow Jesus
Jesus used the word *mathateuō*, or "make disciples" to describe evangelism. "Go ye therefore, and make disciples" (Matt. 28:19 NIV), means to bring people to a conversion experience to become lifelong followers of Christ. Jesus' use of this term may be the only use of the verb in the New Testament.

Pĕithō - Persuading those who are hesitant
The biblical basis of evangelism as persuasion is found in the word *pĕithō*, "to persuade," which means "to bring another to a point of decision." Paul stated, "Knowing therefore the terror of the Lord, we persuade men" (2 Cor. 5:11). When he preached in Corinth, "he reasoned in the synagogue every sabbath, and persuaded..." (Acts 18:4). This does not mean that Christians can talk others into being saved, but that they should attempt, like Paul, to fervently persuade others.

Two doors into the church
In recent years churches have expressed evangelism in several ways but they can all be summarized in two evangelistic strategies—front-door and side-door evangelism.

Front-door evangelism involves inviting and bringing a person through the "front door" of the church to some event or opportunity to hear the gospel. It is also known as *inviting evangelism* or *event evangelism*. This is often done with campaigns and programs to attract large numbers of people to the church and ultimately to the gospel.

Despite the major limitations of this approach, the church has expended most of its evangelistic efforts in this way.

Side-door evangelism, in contrast, is a strategy that attempts to bring people into the church to hear the gospel through personal contact with a church member or attender. This evangelism takes place through the informal contacts that people have everyday. Christians getting to know those in their workplace and bringing them to church represents one example of *side-door evangelism*. Hopefully, the nonbelievers will get plugged into the activities of the church, and through this contact hear the gospel.

Statistically, far more people have come into the church through personal invitations from relatives and friends than by vast advertising campaigns designed to bring them through the "front door" of the church. *Front-door evangelism* is where most of our evangelistic energy is being expended, but it is *side-door evangelism* which is proving more successful in reaching the unsaved for Christ.

Reasons for evangelism

Evangelism is not simply an option for Christians. It is not a responsibility reserved only for those who seemingly have the "gift" of evangelism. It is a mandate for each and every believer and an essential element for living the Christian life. The Bible gives several reasons and motivations for Christians, including the fact that Christ commanded it, that sinners need the gospel, and that love for Christ and for others should compel us toward that task. These reasons and others listed below should cause believers to examine and evaluate their own obedience and motivations in the area of evangelism.

Commanded

Jesus commanded the disciples to "go ye therefore, and teach all nations, baptizing them in the name of the Father, and of the Son, and of the Holy Ghost" (Matt. 28:19). The scope of the command included all nations. The command is also found in Mark 16:15: "Go ye into all the world, and preach the gospel to every creature." This verse makes evangelism personal. The "every" conveys that the emphasis is on sharing the gospel with individuals. This command is directed to all Christians. If you are not helping to win others to Christ, you are not being obedient to Christ's command. Paul felt this compulsion and expressed it in Romans 1:14: "I am a debtor both to the Greeks, and to the Barbarians, both to the wise and to the unwise." He felt the burden of Christ's command to tell others.

Sinner's needs

The lost condition of man compels Christians to evangelize. "For all have sinned and come short of the glory of God" (Rom. 3:23). All men outside of Christ are lost. "The wages of sin is death" (Rom. 6:23). The writer of John declares, "He that believeth not the Son shall not see life; but the wrath of God abideth on him" (John 3:36). If church members comprehended the reality of hell and the severity of God's wrath, they would each dedicate themselves to winning men to Jesus Christ.

Man's seeking for peace compels evangelism. Many seek spiritual peace but never articulate this desire. Jesus has given the invitation, "Come unto me, all ye that labour and are heavy laden, and I will give you rest" (Matt. 11:28). Only the Holy Spirit knows the heart of man (1 Cor. 2:11). Therefore, believers must always be about the duty of evangelism, witnessing to men about Jesus Christ, who offers freedom from the bondage of sin, and peace with God through His death.

Love for Christ

Love for Christ should also be a major motivation for evangelism. Jesus was the outstanding evangelist. He preached God's seeking love and His coming wrath. To Christians, He has given the commandment to prove our love through obedience. "If ye love me, keep my commandments" (John 14:15). Paul indicated that the indwelling presence of Jesus Christ in believers should motivate them to tell others of salvation. "For the love of Christ constraineth us" (2 Cor. 5:14). Christ is concerned about the lost, and since His spirit indwells you, you should be too.

Love for others

Love for others compels evangelism. Men love their families and work hard for them. They provide for their comfort and are concerned during illness. This concern, however, is often not evidenced where their spiritual condition is concerned. The greatest concern of all to a Christian should be eternity. After a conversation with Jesus, Andrew immediately "findeth his own brother Simon, and saith unto him, We have found the Messiah" (John 1:41). The example of Andrew's love should motivate all believers to share the gospel, both to loved ones and neighbors.

The example of Christ and the disciples

The example of the Lord compels evangelism. Jesus continually preached to the multitudes. At other times, He had personal conversations about eternal matters with people such as Nicodemus, the woman at the well, the woman taken in adultery, the rich young ruler, and Zacchaeus.

After Jesus' ascension into heaven and the coming of the Holy Spirit upon the church, the disciples were busy with evangelism. Peter, Stephen, Philip, and Paul testified in public places. There were also examples of personal evangelism, such as the conversation with the Ethiopian eunuch, Cornelius, the Philippian jailer, and Lydia. The church of Jesus Christ thrives when evangelism is a foremost concern of Christians.

Gospel stewardship

God has given His people a stewardship of the gospel. The message of salvation is committed to them and they are responsible to dispense the gospel according to God's directives. In the New Testament, a man who supervised an account for another was called a steward. Paul likens believers to stewards. "Let a man so account of us, as of the ministers of Christ, and stewards of the mysteries of God" (1 Cor. 4:1). God loves men, but more than this, He trusts them with His good news. This responsibility can only be fulfilled through evangelism.

Glory of God

The glory of God compels evangelism. Jesus challenged His disciples to bear fruit (John 15:1-8). Bearing fruit brings glory to God. One example of bearing fruit is winning men to Christ. As an apple tree is expected to bear apples, so Christians must be producing fruit in their own lives. Bearing fruit can also apply to character—the fruit of the Spirit. If Christians are bearing the fruit of the Spirit (Gal. 5:22), they will attract others to Christ. Either way, the work of evangelism is being done and this glorifies the Father.

Lack of workers

Few believers are witnessing. More must obey Christ's command to evangelize. God expects all Christians to be doing this. Their sinful nature, however, makes them hesitant to obey. Christ said, "The harvest truly is plenteous, but the labourers are few" (Matt. 9:37). Evangelism should be a primary emphasis of the church. As the church strives to bring believers to maturity, neglecting the process of evangelism will surely hinder the process. Social action, fellowship, and community service are secondary concerns. A church that is not evangelistic will quickly become ingrown and immobile. Each member must be encouraged to make evangelism an integral part of daily life.

Promise of reward

The promise of reward encourages evangelism. Paul reminds the Christians at Corinth that they must all "appear before the judgment seat of Christ" (2 Cor. 5:10). Next he reminds them that knowing the "terror of the Lord, we persuade men" (2 Cor. 5:11). This persuasion is evangelism. Paul, therefore, witnesses and attempts to bring men to Christ. At another place, Paul indicates, "Fire shall try every man's work of what sort it is" (1 Cor. 3:13). God will evaluate people's efforts and reward them accordingly. Paul says the people whom he had won to Christ in Thessalonica became his crowns, "For what is our...crown of rejoicing?" (1 Thess. 2:19,20).

Summary

Evangelism is at the heart of church ministry. It should not be thought of as an activity divorced from other ministries of the church. Evangelism may occur as readily when the choir sings a song proclaiming the gospel, when a group leader leads a home Bible study, when a pastor invites a response to the gospel message, or when a teacher talks to a child about salvation. Opportunities for evangelism in church ministries are abundant, but evangelism is not limited to activities at church. Evangelism may also occur between two students sharing a lunch at school, or two people talking as they commute to their work-places. Whatever the occasion, Christians must know how to take advantage of the evangelistic opportunities that arise. An understanding of the reasons for evangelism and the different evangelistic methods will be of great benefit. Evangelism is not an elective, it is a divine imperative which every believer must obey.

Notes

1. John R. Mott, ed., *Evangelism for the World Today* (New York: Harper & Brothers, 1938), Introduction.
2. Cited by C. Peter Wagner, *Strategies for Church Growth* (Ventura, CA: Regal Books, 1987), p. 128.

Discussion questions

1. How do the three approaches to evangelism complement each other and represent parts of the strategy of evangelism?
2. Refer to the various Greek words found in the New Testament to describe evangelism. What would be some present-day examples of these different types of evangelism?
3. Define evangelism.
4. List several methods of evangelism prominently used in recent years and evaluate them as "front-door" or "side-door" evangelism.
5. What are some biblical reasons for evangelism?

Application activities

1. Using a chalkboard or an overhead projector, brainstorm and list the types of opportunities to evangelize through the ministries in your church.
2. Discuss the advantages and disadvantages of evangelizing through the church ministries.
3. From a survey of your friends, relatives, associates, and neighbors, make a list of those you could reach for Christ as you learn to share your faith through the church.

USING YOUR
SPIRITUAL GIFTS
IN TEAM EVANGELISM

$$\boxed{2}$$

Three basic facts about spiritual gifts immediately apply to every Christian. First, every Christian has at least one spiritual gift (1 Cor. 7:7). Second, every Christian should know his or her own spiritual gift (1 Cor. 12:1). Third, every Christian ought to be actively using that spiritual gift to serve Christ (Rom. 12:6).

When it comes to evangelism, not everyone has the specific gift of evangelism, but all must be involved in this ministry. Paul indicated that only some have the unique gift of evangelism (Eph. 4:11), but acknowledged that the word of reconciliation was committed to all (2 Cor. 5:19,20). All Christians are ambassadors for Christ.

Believers who have a proper understanding of their spiritual gifts will be able to serve in the area in which they are gifted. More fruitful lives and ministries should result. Rather than make all Christians function as though their primary gift was evangelism, believers should work to understand their place on the team. In this way, they can cooperate with others so the work of evangelism progresses through the various church ministries. Christians should primarily serve in those capacities for which God has specifically and uniquely gifted them. "A man's gift makes room for him, and brings him before great men" (Prov. 18:16). When Christians are all actively involved in using their spiritual gifts, then the church's program of evangelism is strengthened. This can be compared to an athletic team in which every person competes in the position where they have skill and training. The church must work to develop team evangelism as an on-going outreach program in which all believers are on the playing field, actively taking part.

What are spiritual gifts?

Although a much discussed and emphasized subject in church ministry today, spiritual gifts are often misunderstood.

Definition of spiritual gifts

A spiritual gift is a special ability given by the Holy Spirit to enable Christians to serve in the body of Christ. This brief definition addresses three key issues. First, the Holy Spirit is the source of the spiritual gifts. In 1 Corinthians 12:7, Paul spoke of gifts as being "the manifestation of the Spirit," which means they come from the Spirit. Second, "special ability" speaks of their nature. Peter made clear the nature of spiritual gifts when he wrote, "If anyone ministers, let him do it as with the ability which God supplies" (1 Pet. 4:11). A spiritual gift is a special ability given by God. Finally, "service" speaks of the purpose of the gifts. Again in 1 Corinthians, Paul indicated that the purpose of gifts is Christian service (1 Cor. 12:7,25).

The relationship of spiritual gifts to natural abilities

Everyone has natural abilities or talents. Our abilities are the result of the common grace of God. Just as God causes the sun to shine and the rain to fall upon both saved and unsaved alike (Matt. 5:45), so He gives natural abilities or talents to both Christians and non-Christians. Talents have to do with technique, methodology, dexterity, coordination, and other elements of natural power. They are therefore limited in their effect. Natural talent may instruct, inspire, motivate, or entertain; but it cannot render spiritual benefit.

God, however, often allows and enables Christians to use their natural abilities as the means for ministering their spiritual gifts. For example, a Christian who has a natural talent for public speaking may be endowed with the gift of evangelism. By contrast, many others with the gift of evangelism may not be public speakers, but more effective in one-on-one conversations.

Although spiritual gifts are often ministered through the channel of natural talents, the two are distinct and are in no way dependent upon each other. Some Christians have outstanding natural talents that are used by the Holy Spirit in spiritual ministry, while others have spiritual gifts that operate to the glory of God in spite of the absence of natural talents in that particular area.

Spiritual gifts are not the same as the "fruit of the spirit"

The fruit of the Holy Spirit is the mark of Christian character produced in the life of the believer by the Holy Spirit (Gal. 5:22, 23). These characteristics are referred to in direct contrast to "the works of the flesh" (Gal. 5:19-21).

Paul indicated that the fruit of the Holy Spirit works in cooperation with a person's spiritual gifts. In 1 Corinthians 13:1-3, Paul indicated that apart from love, which is one aspect of the fruit of the Spirit, spiritual gifts would be as sounding brass or a tinkling cymbal. Spiritual gifts are special abilities for service, while spiritual fruit is Christian character.

Two kinds of spiritual gifts

Two distinct kinds of gifts operate in the church today: enabling gifts and serving gifts. Enabling gifts are qualities possessed by Christians, rather than activities which they perform. These gifts enable believers to make better use of their serving gifts. Enabling gifts include faith, discernment, wisdom, and knowledge.

Paul seems to say that the enabling gift of *faith* would help a person with his serving gift of preaching (Rom. 12:6). The gift of *discernment* is spiritual insight into people, Scripture, or trends. A believer needs this ability along with the spiritual gifts of *wisdom* and *knowledge* to do a task for God. Every believer may have or be able to develop the enabling gifts and should use them to make their serving gift more effective.

Serving gifts

Serving gifts are God-given abilities for Christian service and ministry (1 Cor. 14:12,26,31) which can facilitate spiritual growth and fruit in the lives of others (1 Cor. 12:7; 14:3,4; Eph. 4:12,16). The following nine gifts might be considered serving gifts. When all are exercised by the entire local church, the individuals become a team for evangelistic outreach.

Evangelism (Eph. 4:11)

The person who has this gift has "the ability to lead people to a saving knowledge of Jesus Christ." Persons with this gift seem to excel in getting decisions for Christ and are often aggressive in pursuing evangelistic opportunities. The strengths accompanying this gift include a consuming passion for lost souls, a desire to improve personal effectiveness through Scripture memory, and a clear understanding of the gospel and its potential for impact. Certain weaknesses can also characterize persons who have this gift. Evangelists may feel strongly that everyone should be an aggressive evangelist and could feel a strong tendency to push for decisions even when people might not be ready. Those with this gift should be aware of the subtle ways pride can develop over successful evangelism experiences. They should resist the tendency to be number-oriented rather than people-oriented.

For evangelism efforts to be effective, it is important that at least some people on the team have the unique gift of evangelism. Others, however, who have gifts listed below are also needed on the evangelism team.

Prophecy (1 Cor. 12:10)
The person who has this gift has "the ability to proclaim God's truth." Most believe that the ability to predict the future (I Sam. 9:9) and to be a channel of revelation (Eph. 2:20) is not operative today. Today, persons with this gift confront, convict, and rebuke. In the exercise of this gift, the prophet "speaks edification and exhortation and comfort to men" (1 Cor. 14:3). The strengths of this gift include a sensitivity to the reputation of God, an ability to quickly perceive and denounce sin, an understanding of people's sinful motives, and a lack of toleration for hypocrisy. This person can communicate directly and frankly, desires to see evidence of conviction, and easily discerns doctrinal issues and church trends. Prophets, however, can often be perceived as harsh and having little concern for individuals. They will need to work to feel comfortable in a discussion-oriented teaching session, may have difficulty in adjusting to others, and may view the sermon as the only means for ministry, thus overlooking many other needs. Struggles with spiritual pride may also plague prophets.

Persons with the gift of prophecy are needed on the evangelism team to convict sinners to repent and to continue to denounce the sins of the flesh once they have believed.

Teaching (Rom. 12:10)
The person who has the gift of teaching has "the ability to accurately make clear God's truth so all can understand it." The strengths of this gift include a desire to study and classify truth, a feeling that this gift is foundational to others, an ability to present truth systematically, a concern for learning, a concern with the accurate communication of Scripture, and lack of tolerance for its misinterpretation. Persons with the gift of teaching have a sensitivity for those who have correct knowledge and an ability to effectively use biblical illustrations in their teaching. Among the common weaknesses associated with this gift are a greater interest in interpretation than application and tendency to emphasize "head knowledge" without relating it to practical faith and living. Those with this gift may fall into the danger of pride about their knowledge, concentrating on details rather than the broader issues of life, or having a greater concern for truth than for individuals.

Those with the gift of teaching are important members of the evangelism team. Many come to know the Lord in the classroom after the teacher has explained the way to salvation.

Exhortation (Rom. 12:8)
The person with this gift has "the ability to stimulate faith in others and motivate others to a practical Christian life." Exhorters are both positive and practical motivators in relating to others.

The strengths of this gift include a tendency to be encouraged by results in the life of another, an excitement over practical principles of life, a tendency to validate all life experiences with Scripture, an ability to be comfortable ministering to both groups and individuals, and a grief over sermons which are not practical. Persons with this gift may have a tendency to want to motivate those unwilling to receive it, be periodically accused of taking Scripture out of context, and could have a reluctance to win souls if follow-up is not assured. These people need to avoid the danger of being discouraged with a lack of progress in listeners, of ministering for selfish purposes, and of ministering to the symptoms rather than people's real problems.

As with other gifts of the spirit, those with the gift of exhortation are needed on the evangelism team to help both motivate persons to receive Christ and to grow in their Christian life after accepting Christ as their Savior.

Shepherding (Eph. 4:11)

The person with this gift has "the ability to serve God by overseeing, training, and caring for the needs of a group of Christians." Shepherds are group leaders. Shepherds have a burden to see others learn and grow, a high sense of empathy and sensitivity, and a strong "others" orientation in ministry. Because of the high degree of concern for others, this person may become over-involved in ministry, have a tendency to become over-protective of people, and could often fail to involve others in service. An individual with this gift needs to avoid the dangers of discouragement, pride, and selfishness.

Many come to know the Lord as a result of being involved in a home Bible study led by a caring, loving group leader—a shepherd. Persons with this gift are often used to bring them into the "fold" and to help them grow through training in the Word of God and to use their newly-received spiritual gift(s).

Mercy-showing (Rom. 12:8)

The person with this gift has "the ability to express special compassion and give spiritual encouragement to those encountering trouble and difficulty." The mercy-shower can empathize with those who have problems and can lead them to recognize the spiritual significance of their circumstances. As well as addressing physical needs, persons with this gift also focus on emotional or spiritual needs, and can have good rapport with individuals as well as groups. Mercy-showers can be perceived as offering help that may not be wanted and as being too intimate with people to whom they are ministering. They may be viewed as tending to attract the retarded, the handicapped, social misfits, and those with emotional problems. Indeed, mercy-showers are uniquely gifted to minister to those individuals who are often rejected or overlooked. Because of an intense compassion, individuals with this gift need to avoid the danger of lacking firmness in dealing with people, basing life on their emotions or feelings, and resenting others who are not sensitive to inner needs.

The Lord often uses times of emotional upset to draw people to Himself and the compassion and empathy mercy-showers give during these times often lights the way.

Serving (Rom. 12:7)

The person with this gift has "the ability to serve God by ministering to the physical and spiritual needs of others." This is also called the gift of helps. Usually, those in the office of a deacon (*diakŏnĕō*) have the gift of serving (*diakŏnia*). The strengths of this gift include enjoying manual projects or practical service, being able to serve without fanfare, sensing physical and financial needs of others, working for immediate goals, and getting satisfaction out of completing projects. Among the weaknesses of this gift could be a frustration with the others' lack of involvement in practical projects. The server's good works might sometimes be wrongly interpreted by others. Individuals with this gift need to avoid the danger of pride, bitterness because of lack of recognition, and being critical of acts of faith that seem "impractical."

Although not often in the front-lines of evangelism, those with the gift of serving keep the program of evangelism moving toward its goals. People are always needed to perform the manual or practical aspects of the ministry and to witness while accomplishing these tasks.

Giving (Rom. 12:8)

The person possessing this gift has "the ability to invest material resources in other persons and ministries to further the cause of Christ." This person feels compelled to give out of a sense of need and has a sincere desire to see ministry grow. Often, givers have the ability to organize their personal lives for financial success, the desire to give quietly and secretly, a sensitivity to quality, an involvement which accompanies giving, and a tendency to become positive role models for others. Among the weaknesses of this gift are that others may feel the person gives for an outward impression, others may feel the person over-emphasizes money and may perceive the giver as being selfish. Individuals with this gift need to avoid the danger of being prideful, of measuring spirituality by prosperity, and of being insensitive to the needs of others because of their apparent lack of personal discipline.

The ministry of evangelism, like many other programs of the church, could not exist without funds and the Lord often moves the "givers" to provide the necessary support.

Administration (Rom. 12:8)
The person with the gift of administration has "the ability to perceive needs, organize, and administer programs, then evaluate the results in light of biblical objectives." This person is a manager or organizer. The strengths of this gift include the ability to see the overall picture and think of long-range objectives, the ability to delegate tasks to other people, a task orientation, the ability to counsel and motivate others regarding a task, and an ability to not be perfectionistic, but to judge a task according to objectives. Because of these people's ability to delegate, others may think administrators are trying to get out of work. Or administrators could appear insensitive to people and inflexible to God's work because they are committed to long-range goals, and may be perceived as glorified bureaucrats. Individuals with this gift need to avoid the danger or becoming power-hungry, using people to accomplish goals (manipulation), or lowering standards to use people for the sake of expediency, despite their character flaws or doctrinal errors.
The success of the ministry of evangelism often depends on people with the gift of administration to organize and supervise.

Gifts produce unity in the body of Christ
Spiritual gifts were intended to unify the church (1 Cor. 12:25). Every Christian has been baptized into (identified with) the body of Christ (1 Cor. 12:13), and has been endowed with at least one spiritual gift (1 Cor. 12:7,11). Because each believer is gifted differently, the body of Christ will be just as diverse as the human body (1 Cor. 12:14). This diversity does not suggest division (1 Cor. 12:15-21). Unity does not require uniformity. God intends that the diverse members of the body of Christ should work together in harmony even as the diverse members of a physical body work together. Each member should complement the other members, because each individual is necessary to the effective functioning of the body (1 Cor. 12:22). Even the Corinthian church was reminded, "Now you are the body of Christ, and members individually" (1 Cor. 12:27). There was great diversity among the members of the Corinthian church, but the diversity of spiritual gifts is intended to unify the local church and to enable the local body to edify itself in love (Eph. 4:11-16).

How to discover your spiritual gifts
The following process has helped believers to determine and develop their spiritual gifts.

Study spiritual gifts
Those who want to discover their spiritual gifts must understand the basic teaching of Scripture on spiritual gifts. Discovery is dependent upon some degree of knowledge. Therefore, a

thorough study of spiritual gifts is the place to begin in an attempt to discover how the Lord has gifted you.

Spiritual gifts inventory

A spiritual gifts inventory may help you discover your gifts. It is based on characteristics of Christians who are known to possess the various gifts. Such an inventory will not give conclusive results, but will indicate which gifts you are likely to possess. One source for these inventories is Church Growth Institute in Lynchburg, Virginia.

Trial and error

One of the most important ways to discover your spiritual gifts is to get busy in the work of the Lord. Your proficiency in an area of ministry may indicate that you possess a spiritual gift. This can be a very rewarding experience, even for those who think they know their spiritual gifts. Trying a new area of ministry may uncover gifts that have gone undiscovered.

Remember, the only people who do not make mistakes are those who never do anything. Those who succeed have usually failed many times. It may be necessary to try many things and fail at several before a gift is discovered and developed.

Consult other believers

Older and wiser Christians sometimes recognize when believers do not have the gifts that they may think or wish they had. Solomon referred to the wisdom of seeking the counsel of others (Prov. 11:14; 15:22; 24:6). Older believers are also often able to recognize and confirm gifts in others that the individuals themselves might not be aware of.

Summary

God has given various spiritual gifts to enable all believers to make use of their individual abilities in the ministry of evangelism. The key to effective implementation of outreach through a church is the discovery, development, and use of spiritual gifts.

Discussion questions

1. Why is it important that Christians know their gifts?
2. What is a spiritual gift and how can these gifts be discovered?
3. What are the enabling gifts?
4. What are the serving gifts?

Application activities

1. Identify which of the serving gifts you think you may have.
2. How could you use your gifts in your evangelism ministry?
3. In what other church ministries should a person with your gifts seek to serve?

FOUNDATIONS
OF
EVANGELISM

$$\boxed{3}$$

The Bible contains principles of evangelism. Both the *message* and the *method* are found in Scripture. Biblical principles are applicable to every age in every culture and should direct the method of evangelism.

The Word of God – instrument of evangelism

The Bible is the record of God's revelation of Himself to His people. It presents the goals of evangelism and provides the dynamic for it. True evangelism must be based upon the Word of God.

Jesus used the Scriptures in conversation with individuals as well as in His teaching. In the synagogue in Nazareth, Jesus was found reading the Word of God. After reading Isaiah 61:1,2, He began to explain to His hearers how the Scriptures were being fulfilled (Luke 4:16-21). Jesus' basic approach to preaching and teaching was an explanation of the Scriptures. After the resurrection, Jesus walked with two of His disciples to Emmaus, "And beginning at Moses and all the prophets, he expounded unto them in all the scripture the things concerning himself" (Luke 24:27). He used illustrations, parables, object lessons, current events, and questions. His purpose was to help the hearer understand the Word of God. Christians today must also keep in mind that their purpose in evangelism is to present the Word of God so that the unsaved may understand and be able to respond.

Christians must clearly explain the Bible to those with whom they are sharing Christ. The Holy Spirit provides the spiritual understanding of the gospel, but He does this through the Word of God. In evangelism, the Holy Spirit uses the Word of God to reach the heart of the unconverted.

21

To convict (guilt feelings)

Conviction of sin comes through the Scriptures. "For the word of God is quick, and powerful...and is a discerner of the thoughts and intents of the heart" (Heb. 4:12). The Word of God exposes the sin that is hidden in the thoughts of man. God already knows that sin is there, but the Word of God convicts by illuminating the mind concerning the sin. It shows individuals how they fall short of God's perfect standard of holiness. But some people have hard hearts. "Is not my word like as a fire? saith the Lord; and like a hammer that breaketh the rock in pieces?" (Jer. 23:29). God can bring conviction to even the hardest heart and cause people to realize their utter depravity before him.

J. I. Packer states that, "To be convicted of sin means to realize that one had offended God and flouted his authority, and defied him and gone against him...".[1] Because of rebellion, man stands condemned under God. Conviction results when people become aware of their wrong relationship with God, and see their further need to be restored to relationship with Him. Packer says further, "Conviction of sin always includes conviction of sins: a sense of guilt for particular wrongs done in the sight of God."[2] We see ourselves as apart from God and, recognizing the result of specific sinful actions, are sorry. "Conviction always includes conviction of sinfulness: a sense of one's complete corruption and perversity in God's sight."[3] Conviction completely disorients a person. A person sharing the gospel can't cause conviction unaided. The non-Christian needs a completely new heart because of the utter corruption and perversity of the sinner in God's sight. Conviction comes through the Word of God, therefore, evangelism must communicate the Scripture.

To convert

The Scripture is said to convert a soul (Ps. 19:7). This conversion results in a changed life in the person. The source of this changed life is the Word of God. The convert makes an about-face and turns to God.

Christians sharing their faith should make sure that the Word of God is understood and communicated. Illustration, rational process, and forceful logic do not win souls. Neither does salesmanship. Only the Word of God can do the work of God in conviction and conversion.

For eternal life

God uses the Bible to give life. When a man is born the first time, he is given earthly life. Jesus said to Nicodemus, "Ye must be born again" (John 3:7). When a person is born the second time, he/she is given eternal life. God uses the Bible as an instrument through which to give eternal life to people. Peter recognized the Bible as the source of eternal life. "Being born again...by the work of God, which liveth and abideth forever" (1 Pet. 1:23). Therefore, it is through God's Word that we receive eternal life.

Jesus is God (John 1:1). When He was upon the earth, He spoke many things. Jesus indicated His words were instruments through which the Holy Spirit could give life, "It is the spirit that quickeneth; the flesh profiteth nothing: the words that I speak unto you, they are spirit, and they are life" (John 6:63). The Word of God gives life, whether spoken by Jesus upon this earth or written on the pages of Scripture.

To cleanse
"Now ye are clean through the word which I have spoken unto you" (John 15:3). The Lord here expressly states that cleansing from sin comes from His Word. Jesus speaks of "abiding in me" (v. 4) as the appropriation of cleansing. Sinners are not forgiven because they hear the Word of God, but because they appropriate it in their own lives. The evangelist, therefore, must communicate clearly the Word in order that it can be understood and applied.

For faith
"So then faith cometh by hearing, and hearing by the word of God" (Rom. 10:17). The Bible is a sure foundation upon which believers may root their faith. Without the Word there can be no ground for faith. But Christians cannot make the Word the foundation of their faith unless they hear and understand Scripture. This message must be received and believed in order for it to be operative in the lives of individuals. The stability of any believer's faith comes from teaching based on the written Word.

To sanctify
Sanctification means "to set apart to God," "to make holy." The Word of God is a means through which Christians are sanctified. Our Lord in His high priestly prayer asked, "Sanctify them through thy truth: thy word is truth" (John 17:17). Christ also gave Himself for the church "that he might sanctify and cleanse it with the washing of water by the word" (Eph. 5:26). So it is, that along with cleansing His church from the guilt and power of sin through regeneration or the washing of water, the Word is also an instrument through which the believer is cleansed from inherited sin and made holy.

This is the dynamic of God's Word. Church volunteers involved in evangelism must know the Word, must experience its power in their own lives, and must be convinced that "it is the power of God unto salvation to every one that believeth..." (Rom. 1:16). All Christians must accept the Word as infallible and authoritative (2 Tim. 3:16). The evangelist speaks forth God's Word, and through it God speaks to the unsaved to enlighten their hearts. No other book can be relied on to change the lives of people. A gospel message based only on persuasive arguments and colorful illustrations is powerless to change lives. The basis of true evangelism is the message of the Word of God.

The Holy Spirit – agent of evangelism

The unsaved are unable to discern the meaning of the gospel. The Scriptures teach that Satan has blinded the unsaved, rendering them incapable of perceiving the good news. "But if our gospel be hid, it is hid to them that are lost: In whom the god of this world hath blinded the minds of them which believe not" (2 Cor. 4:3,4). Because of this, most people do not realize their lost condition. Even when they are warned of the judgment of God to come, they have little concern. An indifferent and neglectful attitude toward eternity is common today. But these unconcerned people must be reached for Christ.

Evangelistic conversations must have a dynamic far greater than that necessary for simple communication of facts. This dynamic is the Holy Spirit. Apart from His ministry, the evangelist's best intention, motives, and methods are futile. The Holy Spirit is the agent of evangelism, making Christians adequate for the task.

For conviction

Before unbelievers can be converted, the gospel must be understood. The Holy Spirit convicts the world of sin (John 16:8). Conviction is more than mental agony or sorrow for sins, although these may follow. Conviction illuminates the mind concerning facts. The Holy Spirit causes sinners to see that they are guilty before God, having broken His laws and come short of His perfect standard (Rom. 3:23). Conviction causes sinners to realize they have not believed in Christ. (John 16:9).

The unsaved will remain in their sinful condition if they reject the Son of God (John 3:18). The main issue for the unsaved is whether they personally accept or reject Jesus. When the Holy Spirit convicts sinners of unrighteousness (John 16:8), He causes them to see Jesus Christ as the only righteous one (John 16:10). Only the work of the Holy Spirit can cause the unconverted to understand that the righteous Christ died for the unrighteous. Unbelievers unaided by spiritual help cannot understand their condition before God, because they do not understand spiritual truth (2 Cor. 2:14).

Finally, the Holy Spirit convicts of judgment (John 16:8). This passage refers to God's judgment on sin at the death of Christ (John 12:31,32; 2 Cor. 5:21). When the Holy Spirit convicts concerning judgment, sinners understand that Christ's death was a judgment upon their sin.

For conversion

Regeneration is the work of the Spirit whereby life is imparted in response to faith. The Scriptures point out that unbelievers are spiritually dead and separated from God by sin. "And you hath he quickened, who were dead in trespasses and sins" (Eph. 2:1). By the miracle of regeneration, the soul is given eternal life. Our Lord describes this granting of eternal life as being "born-again" (John 3:3). The Holy Spirit is the One who gives life to the soul when a person believes and places his/her faith in Jesus Christ. No amount of good resolutions can make a regenerate person. The Holy Spirit must work in the heart as the Word of God is heard and believed. As the new birth takes place, eternal life is imparted. "He that believeth on the Son hath everlasting life" (John 3:36). "Nor by works of righteousness which we have done, but according to his mercy he saved us, by the washing of regeneration, and renewing of the Holy Ghost" (Titus 3:5).

For guiding into truth

When the Word is faithfully proclaimed, the Holy Spirit uses the Word and applies God's message to the needs of non-Christians. As they hear the gospel or Christian teaching, the unsaved are brought in contact with certain truths. People are enlightened through the sovereign working of the Holy Spirit, regarding their sin, Christ's righteousness, and the judgment of sin. "The Spirit places the truth in a clear light before sinners so that it may be seen and acknowledged as truth."[4]

The Holy Spirit is the agent, carrying out salvation in every heart. Halford Luccock has said, "The Holy Spirit is the present tense of God...."[5] God is presently working in the heart and life of every individual through the person of the Holy Spirit. The actual regeneration and subsequent transformation of a Christian will come as God's Spirit moves.

Christians – messengers of evangelism

God uses human messengers to carry the Word of God to the lost. "How then shall they call on him in whom they have not believed? and how shall they believe in him of whom they have not heard? and how shall they hear without a preacher?" (Rom. 10:14). In these verses God speaks of the human responsibility of carrying the divine message.

Their call

Throughout the history of the church, it is clear that God has called and used believers, both professional and volunteer who have been gifted in many areas to carry out evangelism.

God gives people to the church for evangelism. "And he gave some, apostles; and some, prophets; and some, evangelists; and some, pastors and teachers" (Eph. 4:11). God sets aside servants in every generation. God selects these special servants and endows them with a special gift (capacity or ability) of ministry to the church. One of these abilities is the gift of evangelism. Great evangelists fulfill a clear need. These people are gifts of God to the whole church.

But evangelism is not restricted to the evangelist. All Christians should be doing the work of an evangelist. Not all are called to distinctive services, but God's imperative for each Christian is to win others to Christ, "Ye shall be witnesses" (Acts 1:8). Paul exhorts Timothy, "Do the work of an evangelist" (2 Tim. 4:5). Those with the gift of evangelism are to encourage and work together with those who have other serving gifts. None can give excuse for not being involved with evangelism. In the early church "they that were scattered abroad went everywhere preaching the word" (Acts 8:4). Notice the historical situation in Acts 8. Those who went about preaching or telling were not the apostles—the professionals of that time. They were laymen who were scattered from Jerusalem. They proclaimed their faith by word of mouth, on a person-to-person basis. Witnessing is one of the inalienable rights of every Christian. We should not desire a special gift, for we have a special command in the Bible. God commissions us to witness. With God's commands are His enabling gifts. If God has given the command to share the gospel, He will also give the ability to carry out the task of evangelism.

Their importance

Words used in the Bible in reference to believers indicate how important people are to the ministry of evangelism. The following list indicates the relationship of believing and telling others.

Fishers of men – "I will make you fishers of men" (Matt. 4:19).

Witnesses – "Ye shall be witnesses unto me" (Acts 1:8).

Ambassadors – "We are ambassadors for Christ" (2 Cor. 5:20).

Stewards – "Stewards of the mysteries of God" (1 Cor. 4:1).

As ambassadors for Christ, believers should seek out the lost and witness to them about Christ. Every Christian is a steward of God's way of salvation.

Summary

The Bible is the foundation for evangelism. The Holy Spirit's power proceeds through the Word of God. Therefore, evangelism must be carefully based on Scripture, so the Spirit of Truth can cooperate for eternal results.

The Holy Spirit dynamically works in people's hearts to bring them to a saving knowledge of the Lord Jesus Christ. The Bible is the instrument through which God the Holy Spirit operates with convicting power in the unbeliever's heart.

In God's divine program of redemption, people stand as central figures. Unbelievers are to be saved from their sin and thus are the object of grace. Also it is people whom God calls to be the messengers of evangelism and share the gospel message with those who are without Christ. God uses people more than methods in proclaiming the message of redemption.

Notes
1. J. I. Packer, *Evangelism and the Sovereignty of God* (Downers Grove, IL: InterVarsity Press, 1961), p. 61.
2. Packer, p. 63.
3. Packer, p. 63.
4. Roy B. Zuck, *The Holy Spirit in Your Teaching* (Wheaton, IL: Scripture Press Publications, 1963), p. 39.
5. As quoted by Jesse M. Bader, *Evangelism in Changing America* (St. Louis: Bethany Press, 1957), p. 51.

Discussion questions
1. In what ways does the Bible serve as the instrument of evangelism?
2. In what ways does the Holy Spirit serve as the agent of evangelism?
3. Describe how the ministry of evangelism is carried out through people.
4. List several terms by which believers are called which show the responsibility of Christians to share the gospel.
5. What is the relationship of people and methods in evangelism?
6. Evangelists are called fishers of men, witnesses, ambassadors, and stewards. Name several other occupations which might illustrate the work of an evangelist.

Application activities
1. As a group, prepare a statement summarizing this chapter. The statement might begin: "Successful evangelism results from...."
2. Explain how the Scripture, the Holy Spirit, and members of your church are used in various evangelistic opportunities through your church in bringing men to salvation.

CONVERSION
AND
REGENERATION

4

Two terms are used to describe the believer's salvation experience. When viewed in terms of the person's role in salvation, the term used is *conversion*. When considered from God's perspective, people speak of *regeneration*. When we understand these two terms and all they represent, we will more fully appreciate our salvation experience. This understanding is also crucial as we seek to share our faith with others. Many Christians would like to share the gospel, but are hindered because they have an inadequate understanding of what exactly the gospel is and what takes place at the point of salvation.

BORN AGAIN, CHANGED
SAVED,

Definition of regeneration

Regeneration is the work of God through the Holy Spirit by placing in a believing sinner a new nature which is capable of doing the will of God. The regenerated person is capable of doing the righteous things that please God. Regeneration results in more than eternal life, it makes possible our sanctification. Regeneration is the result of that experience which is called being born again. "Therefore, if anyone is in Christ, he is a new creation; old things have passed away; behold, all things have become new" (2 Cor. 5:17).

Regeneration is an act of God

Only God has the ability to save souls. This is evident throughout Scripture. Jonah recognized that "salvation is of the Lord" (Jonah 2:9). Elsewhere, salvation is referred to as the "gift of God" (Rom. 6:23; Eph. 2:8), and Mark points out that no one is able to forgive sin and redeem sinners but God (Mark 2:7).

But it is not adequate to think of salvation as only a legal act

You leads, PRAYS for them them, that all you do.

28

whereby God erases our sins from the legal record. Salvation results in a living, dynamic experience. One of the greatest promises given by God is "whoever believes in Him ... (has) everlasting life" (John 3:16). This everlasting life is more than just a life of endless duration, it is a new quality of life that Christians receive when they accept Christ (John 3:36; 4:14; 7:37-39; 17:3).

Regeneration produces spiritual life

Every person has a living body and soul and at regeneration is given a new nature. Paul reminded the Ephesians, "And you He made alive, who were dead in trespasses and sins" (Eph. 2:1). Jesus said, "I have come that they may have life, and ... have it more abundantly" (John 10:10).

People need spiritual rebirth because they are spiritually dead. Adam was created a living soul (Gen. 2:7). He was alive both physically and spiritually. God warned against eating the forbidden fruit and said, "In the day that you eat of it you shall surely die" (Gen. 2:17). Although Adam ate the fruit and lived physically 930 years (Gen.5:5), he died spiritually the day he ate the fruit. As a result, everyone is born into the world spiritually dead (Eph. 2:1). But when people receive Jesus Christ they receive spiritual life; this is eternal life (John 5:24).

In regeneration, believers not only receive the presence of Christ, but of the entire Trinity. Christ promised that the Father would also indwell believers (John 14:23). The Holy Spirit indwells Christians as well and His presence is the guarantee of new life (Rom. 8:11). Hence, when people are regenerated, they receive the life of God because they are indwelt with the presence of God. The very life of God lives in the soul of believers.

When Jesus told His disciples, "I am the vine, you are the branches" (John 15:5), He was illustrating the unique relationship into which every believer enters at the moment of conversion. The believer becomes one with Christ. Paul often wrote of being "in Christ" and "Christ in you." Both statements are the result of an act that occurred at the moment of salvation.

New nature

When people receive Jesus Christ they become new creations, yet this does not mean the sin nature is eliminated or even transformed. When Paul told the Ephesians to put off "the old man" (Eph. 4:22), he wanted them to recognize that the old nature had been crucified at Calvary (Rom. 6:6). But Paul himself struggled with a continuing sin nature and inability to perform righteousness (Rom. 7:19). While on earth Christians struggle with fleshly desires. But in regeneration, they receive a new nature with new power and new attitudes. This new nature is from the Spirit of God working within them. Now it is the duty of Christians to allow their new nature to direct their life. The struggle between the new nature and the sinful flesh is real. Paul explains that "the flesh lusteth against the Spirit ... so that ye cannot do the things that you would do" (Gal. 5:17). Christians must now walk by the Spirit, according to their new nature so that they will "not fulfill the lust of the flesh" (Gal. 5:16).

New creation – transformation
Paul used this expression when he reminded the Corinthians, "If any man be in Christ, he is a new creature; old things are passed away, behold, all things are become new" (2 Cor. 5:17). God works in believers' lives not just to improve them, but to transform them totally. Paul also described the results of regeneration as a "new man" and urged his converts to "put on the new man, which after God is created, in righteousness and true holiness" (Eph. 4:24).

Changed lives often testify to the reality of regeneration. The Bible teaches that no person is beyond hope. This was certainly true in the lives of the members of the Corinthian church, some of whom were fornicators, idolaters, adulterers, homosexuals, sodomites, thieves, coveters, drunkards, revilers, and extortioners prior to their salvation (1 Cor. 6:9,10). "But," Paul reminded them, "you are washed, you are sanctified, you are justified in the name of the Lord Jesus, and by the Spirit of our God" (1 Cor. 6:11).

When Jesus enters a person's life, a change takes place that only God can perform. Sometimes the change is very dramatic. For others, the change may be slow and gradual, almost unnoticeable without careful observation. But regardless of how it happens, change is inevitable for every true child of God.

Definition of conversion
The human side of regeneration is termed conversion. The apostle Paul described the conversion experience of the Romans when he wrote, "Ye have obeyed from the heart that form of doctrine which was delivered to you" (Rom. 6:17). Conversion does not just involve learning a catechism or knowing doctrine. It embraces the total person which means conversion is related to all three of a person's faculties: the intellect, the emotions, and the will. People must know certain things to experience conversion, but a knowledge of these facts alone will not save them. Conversion also involves the emotions, but it is far more than an emotional experience. Conversion is not complete until an act of the will has taken place, but even an act of the will is not enough to save if it is done in ignorance without a heart desire.

The intellect
A person's conversion to Christ is different from a conversion to another religion or commercial product. Though many have

tried, conversion cannot be passed off as a mere psychological phenomenon.

To be saved, a person must know the gospel. There is only one gospel (Gal. 1:9), but it contains two sides of the same truth. Just as a door has two sides, so the gospel is propositional and personal truth.

The gospel is *propositional* truth, which means it is objective—truth that is accurate. The gospel is the account of the Christ's death for our sins, his burial and resurrection from the dead on the third day (1 Cor. 15:1-4). Only Jesus could provide salvation for us. "But God commendeth his love toward us, in that, while we were yet sinners, Christ died for us" (Rom. 5:8).

A second aspect of this gospel is *personal* truth. When Paul came to Corinth to preach his gospel, he "determined not to know anything among you, save Jesus Christ, and him crucified" (1 Cor. 2:2). The gospel is not complete in its presentation until it focuses attention on the person of Christ. Jesus said, "As Moses lifted up the serpent in the wilderness, even so must the Son of man be lifted up: That whosoever believeth in him should not perish, but have eternal life" (John 3:14,15). If a person does not trust in Christ, that person is not saved. It is important that we know both the content (doctrine) and the person (Jesus Christ) of the gospel to be converted.

Knowing the propositional truth of salvation is knowing God's plan of salvation. A person wishing to become a Christian must follow God's plan. This is sometimes called the Roman Road of Salvation since the verses that are often used to lead a person to Christ are all found in the Book of Romans.

The Roman Road of Salvation
1. Know your need (Rom. 3:23) *Do you know?*
2. Know the penalty (Rom. 6:23) *Do you know what will happen?*
3. Know God's provision (Rom. 5:8)
4. Know how to respond (Rom. 10:9)

The first step in this plan is to know your need. The Bible says, "There is none righteous, no, not one" (Rom. 3:10). This does not mean there is nothing good in people but rather that none of us are as righteous as God Himself. God has a perfect standard of holiness required for entrance into heaven. Unfortunately, "all have sinned, and come short of the glory of God" (Rom. 3:23). It makes little difference how good we are. We are not good enough. If marathon runners attempt to set Olympic records, it makes little difference if they miss by five seconds or five hours. They have missed the standard they had set for themselves. Even if we were "almost perfect," we would still fall short of God's holy standard of perfection.

The second step is to know the penalty. The Bible says, "The wages of sin is death" (Rom. 6:23). Because God is just, He must punish sin. He will "by no means clear the guilty" (Exod. 34:7). His righteousness demands a payment for sin and, as Romans says, the wages of sin is death. This refers to both physical and spiritual death. Physical death occurs upon the separation of a person's body and spirit (James 2:26). Spiritual death occurs when one is eternally separated from God (2 Thess. 1:8,9). John wrote of a future point in time when "death and hell were cast into the lake of fire. This is the second death" (Rev. 20:14).

A third step in God's plan of salvation is to know the provision. This provision is found in the gospel. "While we were yet sinners, Christ died for us" (Rom. 5:8). Because we could not pay the price for our sins, Jesus did. Christ died to bring us to God (1 Pet. 3:18), and today he provides salvation as a free gift to all who will take it (Rom. 6:23). Jesus provided what we could not provide for ourselves. That provision gives us the option to receive or reject God's gift of eternal life.

People can know the above three steps in this plan and never be saved. They must personally respond. "That if thou shalt confess with thy mouth the Lord Jesus, and shalt believe in thine heart that God hath raised him from the dead, thou shalt be saved" (Rom. 10:9). Jesus traveled through Israel and offered salvation to his own people, but he was rejected. "But as many as received him, to them gave he power to become the sons of God, even to them that believe on his name" (John 1:12). You must know how to respond to the gospel and then respond to be saved.

The emotions

Many religious groups place too much emphasis on people's emotions and create what is known as "psychological conversions" to their particular religious sect. In reaction to this, some conservative Christians have attempted to deny their emotions completely. Neither emphasis is correct. God made man complete with an emotional capacity. If kept in proper perspective, our emotions lead to a healthy conversion. The abuse of emotions by some radicals should not cause us to abandon that which is good. It is natural to be emotionally affected by conversion at some time.

The apostle Paul rejoiced "not that ye were made sorry, but that ye sorrowed to repentance; for ye were made sorry after godly manner.... For godly sorrow worketh repentance to salvation not to be repented of: but the sorrow of the world worketh death" (2 Cor. 7:9,10). Paul recognized there were two kinds of emotional reactions to the gospel: "godly sorrow" and "sorrow of the world." "Godly sorrow" has a place in our lives in that it leads to further spiritual insight. The "sorrow of the

The Roman Road Scriptures

Romans 3:23 – Know your need

Romans 6:23 – Know the Penalty

Romans 5:8 – Know God's provision

Romans 10:9 – Know **how** to respond

NEXT WK – GIVE THEME

Who are you going to Evangelize

I John 1:5, 6

Col. 1:21

world" is remorse for getting caught, not sorrow for the act committed.

Sometimes God will allow persons to experience guilt so they can understand and appreciate forgiveness of sins. Often God must use our emotions to cause us to respond to the gospel. On other occasions, God will use our emotional reaction so He can better deal with us after salvation. When Philip preached the gospel in Samaria and many people were saved, the Bible records "there was great joy in that city" (Acts 8:8). The apostle Paul expected his converts to continue to respond emotionally to God. He told the Philippians, "Rejoice in the Lord always: and again I say, rejoice" (Phil. 4:4). It is all right to get excited about our relationship with Christ.

Each of us has a different way of expressing emotions depending upon age, sex, background, and a host of other unique experiences that make us who we are. Sometimes we tend to think the people who shout and jump for joy or who cry loudly are more emotionally involved in a situation than people who sit apparently oblivious to what is happening around them. People are not more or less saved depending upon the volume of their emotional outbursts, but when we are converted, our emotions will be effected to some degree.

The will

God created humans with a will to choose to respond to or reject the work of God in their lives. In order to be converted, people must respond. This does not mean we save ourselves. "For by grace are ye saved through faith; and that not of yourselves: It is the gift of God: Not of works, lest any man should boast (Eph. 2:8,9). While "salvation is of the Lord" (Jonah 2:9) and we do not earn our salvation, God does tell us to receive it (John 1:12). We respond to the gospel with our will when we trust in the Lord (Prov. 3:4), repent or turn from our sins to serve God (Acts 2:38; 1 Thess. 1:9,10), believe the gospel (Acts 16:31), receive Jesus as Savior (John 1:12), call upon God in prayer (Rom. 10:13), and confess Christ as Lord (Rom. 10:9).

Repent and believe

Conversion occurs when people repent of sin and believe the gospel. Repentance was perhaps best described when Paul reminded the Thessalonians "how you turned to God from idols to serve the living and true God, and to wait for His Son from heaven" (1 Thess. 1:9,10). They repented when they turned from sin to the Savior, to serve, to wait. Repentance occurs when people change their mind about sin in such a way or to such a degree that it results in a lasting change in their lifestyles.

But it is not just enough to determine to change. Biblical repentance always involves placing one's faith in God for salvation. Even faith is a gift of God (Eph. 2:8,9; Heb. 2:12). Faith has been described using the acrostic "Forsaking All I Trust Him." Believing the gospel means to depend upon it to be true and effective in your life.

Summary

God is in the life-changing business. He takes the broken pieces of our lives and makes new vessels. Someone has said God takes the canvas of our life when the colors are running and blurring, then paints a masterpiece. God is powerful, and the initiator in salvation, but people must also respond to God's working in their hearts.

God has the power to save everyone today, but He will only save those who call out to Him, acknowledging His holiness and their utter sinfulness. We need to come by faith and as little children trust in Him and be converted. Only then will God perform His work of regeneration in us. We then need to continue to cooperate with God as He perfects that change in us, bringing us into conformity with His likeness and His will.

Discussion questions

1. Define regeneration.
2. List the changes that happen in regeneration.
3. Define conversion.
4. How are our feelings affected in conversion?
5. List some of the responses of the will in conversion.

Application activities

1. Review your own conversion experience. How do you see the aspects of intellect, emotions, and will evidenced?
2. What does a person need to know and do to become a Christian?
3. What are some verses you could use to explain the gospel to an unsaved friend?

HOW TO LEAD
OTHERS TO
RECEIVE CHRIST

$$\boxed{5}$$

One of the greatest joys in the Christian life is leading someone else to receive Christ (1 Thess. 2:19). While not everyone has the gift of evangelism, all Christians can do their part on the team to win others. Therefore, every Christian should know how to lead others to Christ and be prepared to do so as the Lord provides opportunities (1 Pet. 3:15). You can start with those in your sphere of influence: unsaved family, friends, and co-workers.

One key to effectively reaching others for Christ is to establish a common ground upon which you can build. Paul practiced this principle explaining, "I have become all things to all men, that I might by all means save some" (1 Cor. 9:22). This testifies to the fact that most people are reached for Christ through the witness of a friend, relative, teacher, associate, or neighbor. Those in your personal sphere of influence are among the most receptive to you as the messenger of the gospel and may be among the most responsive to its message. If there are no non-Christians in your personal sphere of influence, you must be prayerfully seeking opportunities to be involved in relationships with unbelievers.

A second key in leading someone to receive Christ is to be sensitive to the leading of the Holy Spirit. The Holy Spirit is working in the life of the unsaved, convicting of sin and drawing them to Christ (John 16:8). When we are sensitive to the leading of the Spirit in our life, He will guide us to those who are ready to respond and help us know how to approach them.

A third important key in leading someone to Christ is that of timing. You should be careful not to offend people by trying to force a decision when they are not ready to respond. Likewise, do not excuse your procrastination by claiming you are waiting for the Lord's timing. The urgency of the gospel demands one is always ready and eager to share it with another (1 Pet. 3:15).

Turning a conversation to the gospel

Many Christians find it easier to talk about the weather, a problem at work, a current news item, or a recent sports event than to talk to others about the gospel. In many cases, this is because they are unsure how to begin to explain the gospel without offending someone. Several categories of questions are effective in turning conversation to a presentation of the gospel.

Questions about Heaven

You can change the direction of a conversation by asking a question which calls for a response from the unsaved person with whom you want to share the gospel. Two questions made popular in the "Evangelism Explosion" program are, 1) "If you were to die tonight, do you know for certain that you would go to heaven?" and 2) "If you were to die, and God were to ask you, 'Why should I let you into my heaven,' what would you say?"[1]

The first question introduces the concept that we can "know for certain" about our eternal destiny. The answer to the second question reveals any misconceptions a person may have about how one gets to heaven. It also starts the person thinking about their own justifications for being worthy of heaven.

Questions about a relationship with God

In some cases, people are not as concerned about eternity as they are about a relationship with God now. This is especially true of young adults who are relational in their orientation and are beginning to encounter problems in life bigger than themselves. A question which some people find useful in introducing a gospel conversation is, "If it were possible to have a personal relationship with God, would you be interested?" This question has been often used in connection with evangelistic religious surveys of a community, school, or military base.[2]

As a result of mass immigration to the western-developed nations in recent years, many people living in North American cities come from a background which is neutral or even hostile toward Christianity. Yet as these people begin living in a new land, they are open to learning about the society around them. Those ministering to the non-Christian ethnic groups in major cities often begin talking to the unsaved by asking directly, "Have you ever thought about becoming a Christian?" While many raised in North America would be offended if such a question were asked, one coming from a Buddhist or Hindu land would not take offense and would often respond with interest.

Following up on an evangelistic contact

One of the best ways to share the gospel with someone is to bring him/her with you to a place where the gospel will be explained. Few people respond to the gospel the first time they hear it, but often they are open to talking about the gospel further after the initial evangelistic contact. This contact may include an evangelistic meeting, an article or tract, a movie or video, or any other contact a person may have had with the gospel. Some questions have been developed to follow-up an evangelistic contact.[3] These questions are 1) "What did you think of the message?" 2) "Did it make sense to you?" 3) "Have you made the wonderful discovery of knowing Christ personally?" 4) "Would you like to know more about how to receive Christ?"

Getting permission to explain the gospel

Once a conversation has turned to spiritual things, you can begin to present the gospel. Explain that the Bible discusses many subjects, but its central theme involves how a person can have a relationship with God. Ask the person if you could take a few minutes to share some Bible verses which explain this central theme. It is best if you limit your explanation to 10 minutes.

Presenting the gospel[4]

Mankind's problem – sin

When a person is motivated to hear the gospel, he/she needs to be confronted with the problem of sin. "For all have sinned and come short of the glory of God" (Rom. 3:23). The word translated "sin" in this verse describes the idea of "missing the mark," or falling short of a goal or objective. If a group of athletes attempt to run a three-minute mile, it is likely that all would fail. Some might run faster than others, but none would achieve the standard set out before them. In the same way, all of us have failed to achieve God's standard of holy perfection. Some of us may do more "good" things than others, but none of us is perfect. God sees us all as willfully rebelling from Him and pridefully breaking the perfect standard He has set.

The consequence of sin – death

Secondly, people need to understand the consequence of sin in their life. Because God is a just God, He must punish sin. "For the wages of sin is death" (Rom. 6:23a). The Bible always views death in terms of a separation rather than the end of life or existence. Physical death is the separation of the person's body and the spirit (James 2:26). The "second death" is the eternal separation of a person from God in the Lake of Fire (Rev. 20:14). Both of these deaths are the result of sin.

When working at a job, we expect to be rewarded for our labor in accordance with the mutually-agreed upon terms of employment. These are our wages. In the same way, everyone will be paid for their work of sin on a coming spiritual payday. God has stated that this payment will be death.

God's gift – eternal life
The rest of the verse in Romans explains the good news, that God offers a free gift of eternal life with Him "wrapped up" in the person of Jesus. "But the gift of God is eternal life in Christ Jesus our Lord" (Rom. 6:23b). The good news of the gospel is that Jesus paid the price for our sin so He could bring us to God (1 Pet. 3:18). He now offers the free gift of eternal life.

Most people understand the concept of a free gift. Often a person gift-wraps something they know a friend or relative will appreciate and presents it to them as an expression of their love. In order to receive the gift, the person takes the whole package. In the same way, God offers the gift of eternal life packaged in Christ Jesus our Lord.

Receiving Christ by faith
If receiving eternal life involves receiving Christ, it is important to know how to receive Him. The primary verse in Scripture that addresses this is John 1:12: "But as many as received Him (Jesus), to them He gave the right to become children of God, even to those who believe in His name." Each person must individually go before God with a repentant heart and receive Jesus by faith.

If someone offered you a chair as you entered a room, you would have to consciously decide whether to accept or reject the offer. If you decided to accept, you would sit in the chair and believe it was capable of holding you. In the same way, when God offers eternal life in Jesus, one can only receive it by believing God and putting faith in His promise to save us through Jesus.

Inviting a person to respond to the gospel

Evangelism involves more than explaining the gospel. To be complete, a presentation of the gospel must include an invitation to respond. Before asking the person to respond, be certain that he or she understands the message you have presented. You may want to ask, "Do you have questions about what we discussed?"

Explaining Jesus' appeal to respond
If the unsaved person understands the gospel, one of the best ways to invite a person to respond positively is to use Jesus' own appeal to the church at Laodicea. "Here I am! I stand at the door and knock. If anyone hears my voice and opens the door, I will go in and eat with him, and he with Me" (Rev. 3:20, NIV). Explain that Jesus makes this kind of appeal to everyone as He asks to come into one's life.

When you hear a knock on your door, you can respond in a variety of ways. You can ignore the knock or tell the person knocking to go away, or you can invite the person to come into your home. When people hear Jesus knocking on the door of their lives, they have to choose how they will respond. While you may want them to respond in a certain way, ultimately they must make their own decision for Christ. You must also trust that the Lord is in control. He is the one who opens people's hearts to the gospel. You must trust Him that He will prepare them to receive the gospel in His time.

Leading a person to respond positively

You may want to ask, "Have you ever received Christ and asked Him to come into your life as I explained?" Many believe they receive Christ when they perform church liturgy, but if you explained the gospel clearly, even they should be able to answer this question clearly.

A second question you may wish to ask at this point is, "Is this something you would like to do?" Often, a person will indicate a willingness to receive Christ as Savior at this point, but occasionally he or she may raise an objection. Review or explain any parts of the gospel that may still be unclear. If a person is not ready to receive Christ, be sure you leave the door open to follow up this contact. Often a person simply wants time to think about it and would be open to discussing the matter later.

When people are responsive to the gospel, spend time making sure they really understand this commitment. You may want to ask, "Why do you think you need Christ in your life?" If it seems clear that they understand the gospel, invite them to pray and receive Christ at that time. You may want to say something like, "Why don't we pray together right now so that you can ask Jesus to come into your life? If you want to receive Christ, I can lead you in a prayer to help you express this desire to God."

Praying to receive Christ

Bow your head and begin leading the person in a prayer to receive Christ. Ask him/her to pray aloud repeating each phrase after you. As you pray, use simple language perhaps words similar to these: "Dear Lord Jesus, Thank you for loving me enough to die for my sins. Please forgive me for my sins and save me as You promised. I now receive you as my Lord and Savior. Come into my life and take control. Help me to live for You. I ask this in Jesus' name. Amen."

After you lead in prayer, help the person to understand what has taken place by asking, "Were you sincere when you prayed? If so, did your receive Jesus as your Lord and Savior?" If you have explained the gospel clearly and the person responded affirmatively to Christ, he or she should be able to answer these questions and begin to understand what has happened.

Follow-up begins now

Jesus commissioned His followers to "make disciples," not simply to make decisions. The decision to receive Christ as Savior is the beginning of a life of discipleship. If God gives you an opportunity to lead someone to Christ, you will want to help that person grow as a Christian. Your initial follow-up of this new believer begins even before you part company after presenting the gospel.

Be sure the person understands what has happened
Be certain the person understands what has taken place in his or her life by sharing a verse of assurance. You may want to draw his/her attention to one of several promises in Scripture. If one believes and confesses, then one will be saved (Rom. 10:9). If someone hears and believes the gospel, that person has (present tense) eternal life (John 5:24). The way to determine if one has eternal life or not is to determine if he/she has received Jesus or not (1 John 5:12).
Some people feel different when they receive Jesus, others do not. How one feels is to a large extent dependent upon his or her personality type. Feelings come and go and can be influenced by a variety of factors, but nothing can change God or His desire to have a personal relationship with people. Explain to the person that our relationship with God is based on what He did for us and our response to that, not on the way we may feel.

Invite the person to attend church with you
Jesus established the church as an agency to help individual Christians continually grow in their Christian life and witness. (Heb. 10:24,25). Explain the importance of being with other Christians as they grow in their Christian life. Invite them to attend the next meeting of your church, Bible study, or fellowship group with you.
Remind the person that he or she should not be embarrassed about his/her new relationship with God (Rom. 10:11), but rather should be eager to be a witness for God (Acts 1:8). Encourage him/her to begin telling others about this decision. This may involve responding to a public invitation in a church service, arranging to be baptized, identifying publicly with a group of Christians, and/or talking to others about Jesus.

Continue nurturing the person in discipleship
Remember, if God uses you to help in the spiritual rebirth of another person, make yourself available in the coming weeks to this new believer as he or she struggles with sin in the Christian life. If you cannot be personally responsible for this person's discipleship, be sure to find someone who can fulfill this important ministry.

Summary
Understanding how to lead someone to Christ will help you be more effective in reaching your friends, relatives, associates, and

neighbors. While there may be a tendency to ramble when sharing with others, following a plan such as has been explained in this chapter will help you present the essence of the gospel clearly and give the person the opportunity to respond to the gospel. Nothing is more fulfilling to a Christian than to be instrumental in leading someone to Christ.

Notes

1. D. James Kennedy, *Evangelism Explosion* (Wheaton, IL: Tyndale House Publishers, 1972), p. 22.
2. Religious surveys have been prepared as evangelistic tools by several organizations including Word of Life (Scroon Lake, New York), Campus Crusade for Christ, and the Evangelism Explosion program.
3. These questions appear in Campus Crusade literature and are discussed in their Lay Institute for Evangelism.
4. There are many other plans one might use in sharing his/her faith with a friend including "the Romans Road" (see chapter 4) and "The Four Spiritual Laws" by William R. Bright, available from Campus Crusade for Christ.

Discussion questions

1. What are two questions about heaven you could ask to begin sharing the gospel with a friend?
2. How would you turn a conversation toward the gospel after attending an evangelistic meeting with an unsaved friend?
3. What are four verses you would use to explain the essence of the gospel completely?
4. How would you use Revelation 3:20 to invite a friend to respond to Christ?
5. What are some things you should address soon after you lead your friend to Christ?

Application activities

1. How much contact do you have with non-Christians? Brainstorm ways that you could begin building relationships with non-Christians throughout the daily events of your life.
2. Roleplay sharing the gospel with another class member. The person is an unbeliever who asks you how to become a Christian. What would you say?
3. Write out your testimony briefly (two or three minutes) to share on occasions when you do not have time to explain the gospel completely. Share your testimony with a Christian friend and ask him/her to help you polish it.
4. Make a prayer list of those in your sphere of influence you could share the gospel with. Ask God to help you present the gospel to someone this week.

SHARING
THE GOSPEL
WITH CHILDREN

6

Children face many barriers to salvation. They need adults ready to give Christian guidance. And, more importantly, they need people who are able to lead them to Christ. The Lord loved children for He said, "Suffer (or allow) little children to come unto me, and forbid them not: for of such is the kingdom of God" (Luke 18:16). Those who love children as Jesus did will bring them to the Savior.

Children need Christ

A child will accept or reject Christ. The Bible states that they are born as sinners. "Surely I have been a sinner from birth, sinful from the time my mother conceived me" (Ps. 51:5 NIV). Children will at some point be accountable for the same consequences of sin as adults are. Thus, they are desperately in need of the gospel. Children, like adults who do not know Christ, naturally choose evil and turn from God. It is not easy for them to disregard many wrong influences which clamor for their attention and interest.

As these negative attractions on children are recognized, the importance of evangelism becomes more apparent. To counteract the attraction of sin, children need adult companionship during the crucial years of childhood. They need love and security. They need care and discipline. They especially need the influence of godly parents. But parents often lack Christian conversation, literature, and teaching in their homes and so become dependent upon the church to tell their children of Christ.

The importance of evangelizing children

When the disciples discouraged bringing children to Jesus, He rebuked them and encouraged children to come (Mark 10:14). Matthew 18:1-14 emphasizes child evangelism. Children are given as examples of humility. They are not to be offended (v. 6), are not to be despised (v. 10), and it is the will of the Father that they not perish (v. 14).

The young child who is won to the Lord has a total life potential to be used in God's service. Not only is a soul saved but a life of service to God and to other people is conserved.[1] One evangelist was asked how many people received Christ in a meeting. "Three and a half," was his reply. "Oh, you mean three adults and one child," was the response. "No, three children and one adult. For the children have their whole lives before them, the adult only has half a life left."

Many homes have a growing child with all the potentials for good or evil. That child must be given an opportunity to accept the Lord. If the church has an active program to reach children for Christ, the home as well as the child is helped. The church that takes time for children will usually find a home that has time for the church.

Grouping for evangelism

Often the question is raised, "At what age is a child able to accept Jesus as Savior?" This varies from child to child. The Word of God teaches that children can learn about God, Jesus Christ, and other foundational truths while quite young. "That from a child thou hast known the Holy Scriptures, which are able to make thee wise unto salvation through faith which is in Christ Jesus" (2 Tim. 3:15). So children must be exposed to the message of God's Word, and taught that God is love. They must be taught that people are by nature sinners and predisposed to turn away from God. They must be taught that God is holy and cannot accept sinful things. Such teaching nurtures the child to respond to the claims of Christ during the early years.

Some experiences which prepare children to accept Jesus are worship periods, Christian education classes, Bible reading, conversations about spiritual things, prayer, and singing of Christian songs both at church and home. Also, the radiant and godly life of parents, teachers, and other significant adults exerts a strong influence. Children may not remember all that is said but they will never forget your example and friendliness.

The best time to bring a child to the Lord is when he/she has been spiritually prepared by the Holy Spirit and emotionally and mentally readied by the adults in his/her life. Pray that the Holy Spirit will make you sensitive to a child's need and prepare his/her heart to respond to the gospel. Try to be alert to the time when a child becomes conscious of sin and feels the need for expressing remorse. Direct that repentance to the Lord. Take advantage of teachable moments when the events of life lead the child to a curiosity about spiritual matters and the gospel. A child's decision should be recognized even though he/she previously made one. God's working in the heart is not limited to the plan of a teacher or parent.

Church educational programs are often graded by ages so that students' needs are similar and more effective teaching can result. Evangelism is another good reason for age grouping. Evangelistic emphasis can be more effective when geared to those of the same age group. The descriptions below should be kept in mind by all who work with children, whether parents, friends, teachers, or pastors. Understanding all the qualities of children at different ages is crucial to understanding how to evangelize them.

The *nursery ministry (birth to 2)* should provide an organized outreach of the church into homes where there are new babies. Each year many parents in a community can be reached with the gospel through an organized nursery program. It is an opportunity to reach a home that is ready for the gospel because of hearts warmed by the experience of new life. Even at this early age, newborns and toddlers can be prepared for the gospel by experiencing the protection, comfort, security, and love offered by their parents and other caregivers. Experiencing and learning to trust in this love will help them understand God's love at a later age.

Gear the *preschool ministry (ages 2-3)* to evangelism. The preschool department has a unique ministry to children. Here children learn that the church is God's house, that God loves them, that the Bible tells of God, and that they should love God. These tremendous concepts can be learned early in life and prepare the child for a salvation experience. The preschool ministry has a further evangelistic contribution. Many fathers and mothers will attend a Sunday school or church where there are facilities for their children. They are more likely to respond to the gospel when they can listen to a sermon without the interruptions of small children.

Four- and five-year-olds are at an important age. Some people believe they are too young to be converted. Others feel that children at this age can know they do wrong and that when people realize that they sin, they are old enough to receive Christ. The adult working with children must be careful to be led by the Spirit in personally dealing with children about salvation. Don't minimize the response of small children. A display of faith by the small child is great in God's sight. Because some come from Bible-teaching homes, they are aware of God. Others have no concept of God in their lives. All are old enough to love and/-or honor God, pray to God and, in their own way, serve God.

Six- to eight-year-olds can place their faith in Christ. They realize that they have sinned and often are ready to respond to the gospel. Small children find it easy and natural to trust Jesus as Savior. For those who do not experience conversion at this time, these years can be a time to lay vital groundwork. An effort should be made to lead them in a knowledge and conviction of sin and ultimately to personal acceptance of Jesus Christ.

Many feel that *nine- to eleven-year-olds* are at the best age for evangelism. Surely most have an awareness of accountability and recognize a need to respond to the gospel. Adults working with children of this age must present an evangelistic challenge, as this is quite appropriate. The adult should guard against pushing children. As with conversion itself, the children will require considerable instruction in matters of baptism, ordinances, and church membership. Care should be given to the meaning of these obligations and responsibilities.

Presenting the gospel

Presenting the gospel to children takes prayerful preparation and thoughtful expression. Children should not be expected to apply to their lives a truth which adults have not first applied to their own. Additionally, the degree of personal counseling involved would suggest that a private discussion most often will be the best atmosphere for leading a child to Christ. Adults attempting to lead a child to Christ should be sensitive to these opportunities at home, at leisure, as well as during church programming.

In presenting the gospel to children, language must be simple and on their level. Theological or biblical words should not be taken for granted, but explained plainly. Most church educational curriculum materials provide a glossary of terms graded to children's vocabulary. These can be helpful to any adult wishing to lead a child to Christ. Some modern translations and paraphrases which attempt to place gospel truth in easily-understood terms are often useful in teaching children. Unclear terms often must be explained many times. Some words or expressions that are difficult for children are sin, everlasting/eternal life, saved, died for our sins, receive or accept Christ as Savior, confess, sinner, forgiveness, God's love. Listed below are the fundamental facts that explain the gospel, together with several definitions you might need to provide to children to help them understand:

- God loves you (John 3:16)
- All have *sinned* (Rom. 3:23)
- Christ died for your *sin* (I Cor. 15:3) *Sin = a word, thought, or act against the law of God.*
- *Believe* Christ died for your sin (John 1:12) *Believe = accept as being true.*

- If you *confess* your sin you will be *saved* (Rom. 10:9) *Confess* = *admit that something is true; saved* = *rescued from sin and its punishment.*
- When you believe, you receive *everlasting life* (Rom. 6:23) *Everlasting/eternal life* = *living with a new help from God, will never end.*

Illustrating these concepts using the fingers on one hand will be explained later in this chapter.

The underlying motive and universal language which a child understands is love. When you share with a class of children or an individual child, your non-verbal language must say, "I love you." Your looks, actions, attitudes, and words must radiate love from the Lord. While a knowledge of child psychology may be helpful to successfully work with children, there is no substitute for love.

Public invitations

Giving a public invitation to children should be attempted only with extreme caution and under limited situations.

The cautions

First, children are taught to obey parents and other adults in authority, so they may do what the "adult up front" asks of them. As a result, the response may be focused more on the leader than on the Lord.

Second, children are influenced by peers; they may express a desire to be converted because their friends are doing so.

Third, young children have tender hearts so using stories which play on the emotions during a public invitation to accept Christ (i.e., stories of danger, death, or loss of parents) may prompt an outward response. The adult must be careful that decisions made by children are properly motivated and are centered on faith in Christ.

The situations

Even though these concerns exist there may still be limited situations when an adult may determine a public response would be beneficial. One might be that the group is large and time doesn't permit a personal interview with all. Another may be that a teacher feels compelled to pause in the middle of a lesson and invite children to accept the Lord. Occasionally, but not preferably, the leader lacks confidence to talk personally with his/her students about Christ. In all situations, the guidance of the Holy Spirit is available to those who seek and will follow Him. Group size, time restraints, or insecurities of the leader should never prevent him/her from taking necessary measures toward a conversion experience. If collective counseling is deemed necessary, use the following guidelines.

First, when talking with children who respond in a general evangelistic meeting, it is necessary to determine the basis of their faith. Faith (belief and trust) must be in Jesus Christ, and not in anyone or anything else. Children can have a subjective faith that comes from desire; particularly the desire to please. While this is not saving faith, it can provide an opportunity to make clear their need to trust in Christ.

Second, an open invitation should be accompanied with a plan to meet privately afterwards with each one who responds. During this time, the adult can better review the plan of salvation.

Third, children should be instructed to bow their heads and close their eyes. This can help assure a reverent atmosphere and a measure of privacy and sincerity for the child responding.

The invitation should not be too easy or difficult. If the request has no meaning to the children, the response could be without a change of heart (such as a show of hands). If the invitation is too difficult, timid children might be discouraged. Decisions should not be forced. Reluctance to respond may be because the child does not understand the request or is simply not ready at the moment.

Personally explaining the gospel

Adults leading young children to Christ should use simple ways to illustrate Scripture verses when explaining the plan of salvation. For example, an effective method for illustrating John 3:16 is explained below. John 3:16 divides conveniently into five phrases. They are as follows:

1. God so loved
2. the world
3. that He gave His only begotten Son
4. that whosoever believeth in Him
5. should not perish but have everlasting life.

A simple plan is to let each finger on your hand represent one part of God's great plan of salvation.[2] Let the thumb represent Christ. Most children will be able to understand how the thumb helps pick up objects. In a similar way, Christ helps believers live the Christian life.

As you touch the thumb to the middle finger (representing God's love), you might discuss the expression of God's love as being the center of His plan. God created all things, and He made each boy, girl, man, and woman. He loves each one.

The index finger can represent the world. Each child is one of the people in the world. While touching the thumb to the index finger discuss Christ giving His life for the world. Then separate the thumb and index finger to illustrate how the child is separated from God because he/she is a sinner.

Then touch the thumb to the ring finger and explain that God sent Jesus to give life to those who believe (the ring finger). God sent His Son to die for man's sin. He had no sin Himself, but paid for sin by dying on the cross. But He did not stay dead. He returned to life after three days.

Finally, while touching the thumb to the little finger (representing eternal life) explain that Jesus is now waiting for each child to be saved from the danger of sin. Discuss how eternal life is provided through Jesus. They must believe that He died in their place and is willing to forgive their sin. A turning point from darkness to light is often a brief prayer such as "Dear Jesus, I know I am a sinner, I now believe in You and accept You as my Savior. Forgive my sins and make me your own."

After the child receives Christ

After a child has asked Christ to come into his/her life, a prayer of thanksgiving for salvation should be offered audibly by both child and adult. Encourage these children to tell someone of their decision as soon as possible. It is often a cherished memory so encourage them to write down the date. If children accept Christ privately in church, let them tell the pastor, class members, or friends. If public invitations are given in church, it is good to encourage them to go forward confessing that Christ is their Savior. If you are someone other than the child's parent who has led children to Christ, be sure they share this experience with their parents. If the parents are not Christians, you may offer to go home with the child or call during the week to help explain what happened. Also, follow up by sharing this experience with the pastor.

Adults have the great responsibility of guiding these newly-saved children in spiritual growth.

As with new Christians of any age, newly-believing children must be taught the importance of prayer. They should understand that prayer is talking to God. Since prayer, like breathing, must be regular, they should be encouraged to pray daily giving thanks for their blessings, for guidance, and help from temptation. Opportunity for prayer should also be provided in the various educational agencies of the church. Parents and teachers should take time to establish a habit of prayer with them. They should be enrolled in church activities and introduced to mature Christians in the church who can encourage them in their Christian life which will help to strengthen their Christian walks.

These children must also be taught the importance of Bible reading. Every child should have a Bible and reading guide to follow. Cooperation with the pastor in suggesting materials to be used can help in establishing a church reading program.

Witnessing also is essential for Christian growth. If children are taught how to share their new faith with others, it will be much easier for them to witness later as youth or adults. Sometimes the Wordless Book, which uses different colored pages to depict the steps to salvation, can be used by a youngster. The simple faith and trust of children can be shared with their classmates at school and their companions in the neighborhood.

Summary

Adults working with children have a great responsibility. Teachers and parents must teach Bible lessons faithfully. Teachers should know each child in the classroom well. Being aware of the needs and personalities of all the children will help adults when the Holy Spirit prompts them to speak to an individual child. The examples of adults around them are one of the greatest witnesses for Christ to young children. These adults must know how to lead a child to Christ and be ready to respond to the child's sincere questions about eternal matters. Once a decision is made, the adult becomes a guide to spiritual development so that the one who confesses Christ can grow to spiritual maturity.

Notes

1. David M. Dawson. *More Power in Soul Winning*. (Grand Rapids: Zondervan Publishing House, 1947), p. 58.
2. The idea for using the hand came from Walter H. Werner, "How to Lead a Child to Christ," *Guidelines for Christian Parents*. (Lincoln, NE: Good News Broadcasting Assn., Inc., 1967), p. 12-16.

Discussion questions

1. What is the biblical basis for evangelizing young children?
2. How does dividing children by age help in evangelism?
3. What cautions and guidelines should be considered before attempting to invite children to publicly accept Christ?
4. In what ways can a teacher give opportunity to receive Christ during a lesson period?
5. What is the adult's responsibility after a child accepts Christ?

Application activities

1. Ask a church teacher of children the following questions:
   (1) At what age are children usually brought to Christ in your work?
   (2) How do you lead a child to Christ?
   (3) How are children followed up after they have made a decision for Christ?
2. Request the opportunity to tell a brief evangelistic story to one of the early childhood departments at your church. Discuss with classmates how you should move from the facts of the story to decisions by the children.
3. Prepare a file of child evangelism materials. Include such items as the Wordless Book, children's tracts, lists of available films for children, and devotional aids.

SHARING
THE GOSPEL
WITH YOUTH

$$\boxed{7}$$

The vast potential and the unique problems locked up in youth challenge everyone who ministers to this age level. The adolescent years are often the years of decision. The teenage years are a comparatively small portion of the total life expectancy, but a time when many accept the Lord. Although adolescence is a period of honest doubts and questions, teens are spiritually sensitive and religious awakening is evident.

Responsiveness to love

The way youth act and respond presents a great and continuous challenge to those who work with them. Young people may at times seem unpredictable, melodramatic, cynical, disinterested, or even disruptive. But much of this is a veneer, intended to cover the turbulent, anxious, questioning nature of the growing individual. Although their behavior may convey the opposite, youth have the basic need for love and tenderness that only Christ can provide. In the conversation between Jesus and the rich young man, Mark comments that "Jesus ... loved him" (Mark 10:21). Christ's attitude toward youth in all generations is love. Adults hoping to reach young people must also strive to love them. You must seek to understand the problems confronting today's youth and be sensitive to their struggles. Only then will you be best prepared to present the gospel to young people.

Understanding youth culture

Today's youth are confronted with a world of teenage pregnancy, abortion, suicide, confusion, drug abuse, addiction, and gang violence. Disillusionment, depression, and despair are common. These factors paint a dismal picture for the growing young person, who is also confronted with a changing physical and psychological makeup. Pressures from society, parents, and peers all seem to scream for the young person's attention.

Physical changes
The adolescent's physical development is progressing at a rapid level that often exceeds the emotional and mental maturity of youth. Puberty effects the whole person. For the first time, they may feel self-conscious about appearance, may seem "clumsy" and will have an increased interest in sexual matters.

Psychological change
Emotional changes relating to the ongoing physical changes plague youth. An emotional unrest develops that can cause the unpredictable behavior so characteristic of youth. The young person is faced with questions of how to deal with these new and demanding feelings: "How do I relate to the opposite sex?" or "What do others think of me?"
Because of these heightened emotions, youth are more susceptible to the many elements that bombard the senses. Youth typically spend several hours watching television or listening to music. These and other media significantly impact their emotions and attitudes.

Struggle for independence
Adolescents are in a no-man's land—a buffer zone between childhood and adulthood. They want to be treated as mature people. They do not want others to decide for them, but want to make their own decisions. They feel compelled to reject the attitudes handed down from parents, but feel insecure and apprehensive about how to form their own opinions.

Peer influence
Parental and adult influence on youth steadily declines as the adolescent becomes older. Values and expectations of those in their own age group now become more important. Relationships with peers often become the controlling factor in the young person's behavior and attitudes.

Changing societal influences
The youth culture of today is dramatically affected by the changing society around them. The breakdown of the traditional family unit has seriously affected teenage values. Many now come from divorced or single-parent families and lack a degree of security that once was synonymous with family life.
Drugs and sex have become pervasive elements of society. Young people feel pressured by a world in which birth control is readily available and drug use is common among peers.

The "me-ism" culture of the last few decades has filtered down to the youth as well. They see material success and financial gain as barometers of a successful lifestyle.

"Who am I?" – stepping stone to conversion

Youth are seeking personal identity. "Who am I?" is the inner question of the young person. Throughout the years, self-identification psychology has been rising. Psychologists have found that youth go through an identity crisis as they develop. Identity is a quest among youth. They want to be accepted as persons. They are bombarded with the "Who am I?" question at school, in teen literature, on television, and through many other forms of media. The Bible has an answer for this and adults seeking to share the gospel with youth can move from this self-identity concern to a presentation of the gospel. Parents and teachers of youth must strive to help young people see themselves as the Bible sees them.

A sinner

Whether subjectively felt or not, youth are sinners. This sinful nature must be viewed and interpreted for what it is—rebellion against God. In seeing themselves as sinners, youth are on the road to understanding salvation.

A loved individual

No single additional factor can contribute so much to a youth's sense of self-esteem as to be loved unconditionally (John 3:16). God in love has a plan for each life which is in the best interest of that person, and in love He will enable a young person who comes to Him to fulfill that plan.

A deciding person

During childhood most major decisions were made for the young person. With the end of adolescence, youth are faced with choosing a mate, a career, and a role in life which will bring personal satisfaction. But the individual alone must make these choices. Youth desire to be self-determining individuals. They demand the right to choose their own clothes, their own friends, and their own means of happiness. Their greatest choice, although they might not realize it, concerns heaven and hell. They must make that choice for themselves. In this grave responsibility of choosing between life and death, however, young people need spiritually mature adults to guide them, to answer their doubting questions honestly, and to lead them to right decisions by accepting the Lord Jesus Christ as Savior and Lord. As Joshua challenged his hearers, "Choose you this day whom ye will serve..." (Josh. 24:15), the adult has a solemn responsibility to present youth with the challenge of salvation.

An accepted person

Teens are concerned about being accepted by peers and adults. They also should be concerned about being "accepted in the beloved" (Eph. 1:6). Teens should realize, "I am one who has been accepted by God, because I know Jesus Christ." Those working with youth must confront them with the obligation of responding to God's provision of salvation before they can be accepted by Him.

Each young person must develop meaningful relationships, for the depth of life's meaning to them is found in friends. If they will become friends with Christ and receive Him, they will establish a relationship with God. Then they can branch out into in-depth relationships with other members of God's family.

Christian youth need not remain with their conflicts indefinitely unresolved. While it is true that we cannot extricate ourselves from sin and problems, God, through the Holy Spirit, can and does produce a transformed nature through the new birth.

The adult must recognize teenage doubts and build a ministry on an intelligent interpretation of the Bible. The parent or teacher should never laugh at their questions, but teach them the difference between criticism and evaluation. When they ask questions that you cannot immediately answer, you must be willing to respond "I don't know." Youth will more highly respect the adult who tries to struggle with them in finding answers than the one who pretends to have all the answers.

One of the ways in which youth can find answers to their problems is through Bible study. Here they find the answer to life's needs—the Lord Jesus Christ. The lives of young people can be changed if they learn to dig into God's Word intelligently, thoroughly, and systematically.

Evangelizing through Bible study

In order to be effective, the adult who is attempting to lead young people to Christ through Bible study needs to deal with several aspects of the process—the assumptions, attitudes, approach, and atmosphere.

Assumptions

The Word of God is the final authority. It is revelation from God that demands a response. Parents and other adults should teach for a decision and seek for teens to respond to the Word. Teenagers should realize that God's Word is not optional—it is essential. The Bible convicts us of sin and leads to transformation of life. Therefore, Bible study is basic for evangelism.

Attitudes

The Bible must be taught to apply to life. Bible study can be meaningful only when directed to the teens' lives.

In the sense that Christ is to be at the center, all of life is sacred. The Bible has principles for all of life and should be related to every need. The Word of God is truth. Our Lord asserted, "Thy Word is truth" (John 17:17). So life must be molded according to the Word of God.

Approach

The adult's task is to guide youth in exploring Scripture. Young people should be encouraged to be directly involved in group Bible study—either church or home-based. The adult can make this activity just as evangelistic as a preaching service. In many ways, this direct interaction with the Scriptures is even more profitable, because it encourages youth to compare the elements of their lives with Bible truths.

Participation in Bible study involves mental and emotional responses. Since youth have the capacity for critical thinking, every class session should be thought-provoking. Resorting to sensationalism or startling remarks is not necessary to get youth to think, for nothing is more powerful than an idea. Learning takes place when people are actively engaged in considering, discussing, analyzing, interpreting, and applying ideas to meet life's needs. In so doing, youth are not only learning facts, but they are building up intellectual and emotional attitudes which will help them make a decision for Christ.

Atmosphere

A Bible study is most effective when participants interact. In an informal setting, the leader needs to involve all the participants in the teaching-learning process and help everyone that cares to to respond. The leader must welcome questions the young people ask. The only thing keeping a youth from accepting Christ may be a question. Questions are evidence of interest. They should be answered from the Word or with a principle from the Word. The effective leader will join in with the youth in the quest for truth.

The environment should be arranged in a comfortable, informal manner. In a classroom, chairs could be moved into circles or around small tables. Discussion is always easier when people face each other. In a home, comfortable sofas or even throw pillows on the floor would be suitable. A comfortable environment contributes to an atmosphere which promotes discussion.

Each young person should have a Bible and use it. The more it is used the more familiar it will become. At times silent reading of certain passages, or guided search for Bible answers to chosen questions, can direct attention to salvation.

The leader can maintain a high interest level in searching Scriptures by making resources known. Books in a church library can provide help. People within the congregation can often provide information youth need as well. Youth who feel at ease discussing temporal problems with some adults will also feel free to share their spiritual questions with them.

Bringing youth to decision

"Reaching youth in time provides them with firm anchorage and steady rudder."[1] Often young people need to face a crisis experience in their lives before they realize that they are actually in rebellion against God. C. S. Norberg expresses this realization of rebellion strongly, "There must be a sin-experience, sin-feeling, sin-despair, sin-deliverance."[2]

As presented in the book of Romans, you must explain the need of salvation (Rom. 3:23), the penalty of sin (Rom. 6:23), God's provision (Rom. 5:8), and the necessity of man's response (Rom. 10:9,10).

Youth must understand that conversion is an experience which includes three elements of the person—the intellect, the emotions, and the will. Conversion includes a voluntary turning away from sin. The first component, repentance, involves:

1. An intellectual element: a recognition of sin as the individual's personal sin and rebellion (Ps. 51:3,7,11).
2. An emotional element: a change of feeling, a heart sorrow for sin, and love for God (2 Cor. 7:10).
3. A volitional element: an inward turning from sin, a renunciation of sin and sinful ways (Ps. 51:5,7,10; Jer. 25:5).

Conversion also involves faith, which is a change whereby the sinner turns to Christ. It involves:

1. An intellectual element: an acceptance of the Scriptures and what they teach about the provision of Christ's death on the cross.
2. An emotional element: a personal assent to the power and grace of God as revealed in Christ Jesus, and trusting Him as the only Savior from sin.
3. A volitional element: a dedication of the soul to Christ and a positive act of receiving and appropriating Christ as the only source of pardon and spiritual life.[3]

After youth accept Christ

Youth need to be evangelized and youth need to be equipped to evangelize. Christian teens need to be grounded in the Word of God if they are to mature. Some will accept Christ and return to homes which know nothing of Him. Church leaders will need to assume some responsibility in nurturing these young people and grounding them in the Word (chapter 11 will be helpful).

One of the best ways to win youth to the Lord is through the witness of Christian teens.[4] Youth should be involved in the church's evangelistic thrust. Activities which can challenge youth are suggested by Edward and Frances Simpson. These are:

Canvassing	Prayer cells	Campus forums
Traveling choirs	Billboard posters	Literature distribution
Gospel films	After-game socials	Hobby or craft clubs[5]
Vacation evangelism		

Gunnar Hoglund suggests many approaches to reach non-church youth. Some of these include:

| Mail evangelism | Telephone brigades | Evangelistic crusades |
| Athletic missions | Resort evangelism | Coffee house evangelism[6] |

Youth have been challenged to prepare and then teach in summer ministries and weekday clubs for children. Youth will respond to a challenge.

Summary

Sharing your faith with young people is both a privilege and an obligation. A person won to Christ while still in their teens has a foundation for right living to build their life on and a set of goals for which to strive. The caring adult can help settle their convictions and loyalties and guide them in life's quest. The church and the home must be involved in reaching, teaching, and winning youth to Christ. Adults must also help teens learn to reach other young people.

Notes

1. Ted. W. Engstrom, "All Out for Youth," Moody Monthly, Vol. 57 (July, 1957).
2. Sverre Norberg, *The Varieties of Christian Experience* (Minneapolis: Augsburg Publishing House, 1937), p. 137.
3. Refer to Augustus Hopkins Strong, *Systematic Theology* (Westwood, NJ: Fleming H. Revell Co., 1907), p. 832-39.
4. Edward D. and Frances F. Simpson, "Evangelism of Youth" in Roy G. Irving and Roy B. Zuck (eds.), *Youth and the Church* (Chicago: Moody Press, 1969), p. 174.
5. Simpson, p. 175.
6. Gunnar Hoglund, "Reaching Non-Church Youth," in 1969 *Workshop Outlines* (Chicago: Greater Chicago Sunday School Assn. 1969), p. 5.

Discussion questions

1. In what ways is adolescence a changing age?
2. How does the Bible characterize youth?
3. How can Bible study contribute to youth evangelism?
4. Discuss ways a converted youth can be helped to grow spiritually. What are some practical examples of this?

Application activities

1. Observe five teenagers in your church or community and make anecdotal records of their actions in expressing self-identity, freedom, activity, and feelings. Try to get one statement in each category for each student.
2. Some teenagers have an early religious experience to look back upon but no confidence that they belong to God. Discuss various ways such a teenager might be helped spiritually.
3. Examine your church's program to determine what it contributes to teenage conversion and spiritual growth.
4. What exposure do you have personally to youth? Discuss with classmates how you could better reach out to those young people you have contact with.

SHARING THE

GOSPEL

WITH ADULTS

$$\boxed{8}$$

When God began the human race, He made adults. Although the Bible clearly shows God's interest in children and youth, the great programs center around men and women. Although young Samuel answered God's voice in the tabernacle and David defeated Goliath as a shepherdboy, leadership in both Old and New Testaments rested with adults. Our Lord trained adult leaders who shaped the course of the world. Today, the divine imperative is for men and women whose lives have been changed by the Lord to reach lost adults for Christ.

Since adulthood covers such a wide age range, in order to understand how to most effectively evangelize adults, needs and strategies are presented in three divisions of adulthood, young (18-24), middle (25-50) recently referred to as Baby Boomers, and older (over 50).

Reaching the young adult

Transition and change best characterize the period of young adulthood, the phase of life which usually lasts from the ages of 18 to 24.

Description of young adults

During this stage, individuals are resolving the final developmental tasks of adolescence and preparing to enter the adult world. Psychologist Daniel Levinson calls this period the early adult transition, the culmination of the childhood era, and the beginning of the first adult era. If Christians hope to lovingly and meaningfully share the gospel with this age group, they must have an accurate understanding of the challenges faced by young adults during this time.

Early adulthood consists primarily of two facets: separating from childhood's ties, and forging a place for oneself in the adult world. Individuals of this age separate in many ways. They may go away to college, move out of their parents' home, begin full-time work, or become independent financially. Young adults become more emotionally and intellectually independent as well. They begin to question the beliefs and values they have been taught as children. They evaluate their parents' lifestyle and assess how theirs will be alike or different.

Erik Erikson, a developmental theorist, has said that these individuals are in the final stages of resolving the search for identity that began with adolescence. Because of this, critical evaluation and individuation is necessary. They question everything in an attempt to establish their own rightful place in the adult world.

At the same time, they begin to encounter the choices, roles, and responsibilities of adulthood. The choice of what career to pursue, what college major to select, where to live, what friends to have, and how to spend money confront the young adult. As they embrace their growing autonomy, they are more receptive to considering various viewpoints and assessing their validity.

Near the end of this period, healthy young adults begin to emerge with a fairly well-defined identity. The life focus now begins to shift from identity to relationship, the primary theme of the next stage of adulthood. The struggle to form intimate, lasting relationships now provides the shaping force in the young adult's life.

How young adults are receptive to the gospel

People between the ages of 18-24 are ripe for the gospel. More people make commitments for Christ during this time of life than during any other.[1] Perhaps the broad restructuring of identity and lifestyle which takes place can account for this receptivity.

Because young adults are still defining their identity, they are not as "closed" to considering the gospel as they will be later in life. They tend to be quite inquisitive and the major transition they are undergoing makes them willing to entertain different systems of thought. If they come from Christian homes, they are ready to test their parents' faith to find out if the gospel does indeed make sense. This is often a time when they "make their faith their own." If they are from unbelieving homes, they probably are interested in exploring different religions and may readily consider Christianity.

Because a central factor of the young adult stage is choice, they will be more open to a call for commitment to Christ. If they do make a decision, they will tend to respond more radically than would those of other age groups. They may more zealously incorporate Christ into their developing identity.

Strategies for sharing the gospel with young adults

As with any age group, an effective evangelism approach for young adults is friendship evangelism. When people have been able to see consistent Christian witnesses and discuss issues spontaneously with Christian friends, they will be more open to a gospel presentation. This is especially true near the end of this stage, as relationships become more important.

Proclamation evangelism and persuasion evangelism also work quite well at this time, when young adults are very willing to discuss matters, even with strangers. Christians should use creativity in reaching this age group. Performing a skit, doing mime, playing a musical selection, or holding a debate in public places where young adults will be often catches their interest and draws a crowd. Afterward, an emcee could explain why you are there and what Christ means to you. Christians in the group should try to talk personally with the non-believers around them and ask if they may quickly share the gospel. Even though the approach is introductory, be genuinely interested in the person. Be willing to talk with them and listen to their questions and concerns. After presenting the gospel, always provide an opportunity to make a decision for Christ.

Young adults are often very interested in apologetics and evidences for Christianity. Those sharing the gospel with this age group should be prepared to answer many questions. Paul Little's *Know What You Believe* and Josh McDowell's *Answers to Tough Questions* and *Evidence that Demands a Verdict* would be helpful for this purpose.

This age group often has more time to commit to activities than older adults, when marriage and household responsibilities claim a larger percentage of free time. Consequently, they might be more open to gospel approaches that demand time. Try inviting them to church activities with you, or offer to hold a series of investigative Bible studies in your home once a week. Remember, doubts and questioning are a normal part of the young adult mindset. Be patient with them, and don't try to stifle doubts and questions, as these help individuals to grow in their moral reasoning capacity. Be a friend and be committed to their growth. In this way, God can best work through you to make His gospel known.

Reaching the middle adult (Baby Boomer)

A generation of children, born between 1945-1964, comprise the "Baby Boomers." However, for this study, we will consider the middle adult category to comprise ages 25 through 50.

Description of the Boomers

The Boomers are unique from other generations of adults which have come before them. They have been described as "the generation which refused to grow up." Still others regard them as the generation which changed the world in this century.

Boomers have unfortunately been considered anti-institutional because of the protests of the sixties. Rather, they are opposed to the hypocrisy and injustices of institutions. As a result, Boomers have been conditioned to frequently evaluate their loyalty to jobs, church, or other institutions. They will commit themselves to any cause if it helps them function in life. Consequently, they want a Christianity that works in the marketplace and is a functional positive experience.

Boomers are a fertile field for evangelism. They are influential and will take over the leadership of the church within this decade. Today, they are the junior executives and middle managers in business. As they are becoming the primary influences, our culture is being molded according to their values and ideals. To reach them for Christ, we must have an adequate understanding of this crucial age group.

Generally, Boomers are experience-oriented in fulfillment and short-termed in value judgment. Experience is their primary test

bout making money than
naterial success. They are
r life, from sports (leisure)

Karen has been discontent with her marriage relationship lately. It seems that she and her husband seldom talk with each other and the spark that was once there is long gone.

spel
stitutions of society; i.e.,
As a result, reaching them
these institutions.
 more the center of the
ellence and attraction to
e toward family. They are
e and parent, seeing still
es such as family violence,
IDS, abortion, and porno-
 they impact the family.
 these and other contem-
gelism.
styles have resulted in less
pend this time with their
 more likely to take their
ips than to save and plan
pportunities that capitalize
d incorporate an entertain-

it is reaching the Boomer's
ey will bring their spouse,
 members. This does not
tries focus primarily on

reaching children and youth. Energy expended in reaching the Boomer is more effective than other expenditures because families, rather than individuals, are receiving ministry.

Boomers often are not loyal to the traditional church. With increased freedom in society to choose what will satisfy them, Boomers tend to seek churches which have innovative services, particularly independent and interdenominational churches. As a result of dissatisfaction with the church of their youth, and willing to cross denominational lines, they are more likely to support meetings of different theological persuasions; sometimes with purposes contrary to their own church.

Like other generations of adults before them, Boomers are returning to regular association with the church for the purpose of teaching values to their children, providing services for their growing families, and relating to other parents with similar goals and problems. As they move into middle age, they are looking to the church for stability. The Boomer's confidence, however, is bolstered by perceived "quality" in their churches. They want things to be as innovative as they see through the eyes of media. Their church, as their homes and workplaces, needs the latest tools for the job. This includes the computer, FAX machine, overhead projectors, VCRs, and regular seminar opportunities. They do not want their church to waste their time. Despite advanced technologies, the Boomer tends to work harder and longer than their parents did. They are driven by a desire to be the best they can. Last year's computer is obsolete to them and what worked six months ago may not be adequate for the next quarter. Many own and operate their own small businesses. As a result, their success or failure in business means success or failure in other areas of life. The Christian business man or woman will continually encounter opportunities for sharing the faith and hope of Christ. Professional Christian fellowships provide excellent bridge ministries. The pressure associated with their business life has introduced a new word into the society's vocabulary—"stress." To counter the negative impact of stress and other lifestyle-related health problems, Boomers read books, join health clubs, attend seminars, eat nutritionally, and experiment with spirituality. But they are still left with an inner insecurity as they realize that they have worked harder and seem to have less satisfaction than their parents.

Strategies for sharing the gospel with Boomers

The worship service can be an effective tool for reaching the Boomer with the gospel, but may need to be adapted to promote more experiential worship. They are looking for functional services that relate to their life and a place to involve their intellect, emotions, and will. They want a conservative yet non-traditional ministry and sermons that give them principles to live by.

Boomers can be reached through the educational ministries of the church, but only if those ministries are committed to teaching principles of life that will make the Boomer a better person. They are accustomed to continuing education courses in other areas of their life; therefore, educational ministries must teach Boomers how to relate to contemporary issues. As a result, they are more likely to be part of a home cell group than listen to a traditional Sunday school class Bible lecture.

This generation is relational! They view the church as a community and support group perhaps as much as their ancestors who settled America. When they look for a church, they are looking for a place where they can become involved with people and find new friends. Research suggests that if Boomers do not become members of a group in the church within two weeks of their first visit, they will likely be lost to that church. The confrontational approach to evangelism, typical of a previous generation, is not effective.

Fellowship is the key to bonding Boomers to the church. Groups formed around areas of common interests such as athletic teams, artistic groups, single parents, etc., are essential to reaching them with the gospel and keeping Boomers in the church. Boomers will come and stay where they are accepted for who they are and can relate to others like themselves.

Reaching the older adult

Older adults, as we consider them in this total setting, are people over 50. Since this is a wide age span, perhaps 20-30 years, much of what we say about this group will be general. Since statistics tell us, however, that the incidence of conversion of adults is reduced as adults age, our focus will be heavily upon the age group of 51 to 65.

Description of older adults

As was identified with the Boomers, relationships remain a focal point of interest for adults of this age level. Several significant changes from all other adult groups, however, must be considered. Most adults at this age are experiencing fulfillment. For many, this fulfillment is positive and enhances self-esteem. Others, however, are finding that their life dreams have not been fulfilled and are having to adjust their dreams to reality.

For example, some older adults find that they have not realistically achieve their vocational goals. Or others may begin to see that their romantic expectation of the ideal family is disillusioning and not happening to them. Others that may have assumed that they would remain as physically fit as they were in their earlier adult years find this is not true. Such changes are not only a reality but an experience with painful emotional overtones.

How older adults are receptive to the gospel
Older adults are simply experiencing change. Changes which they did not necessarily anticipate. Thus, such changes catch them off-guard. These changes are not only vocational, familial, and physical, but societal and philosophical as well. During this period, adults are struggling again to find the meaning of life, somewhat similar to what they experienced as teens.

Older adults often question the values held earlier in life. Skepticism often tells them that what they thought were foundational rocks or anchors for their life have now become shifting sand. Thus, they have a strong need to rediscover truths to live by. These truths, however, are only seen as valuable as they provide answers for the life problems and challenges that they face. They are not looking for theological arguments. They are not seeking new understanding. Only as such experiences produce real insight into life's challenges and problems do such efforts interest them.

Strategies for sharing the gospel with older adults
Evangelization strategies for older adults must be firmly grounded in their needs...as they see them. As mentioned above, these needs are relationships and life-relevant answers. And that is where evangelism must focus in order to be successful with such adults.

Therefore the strategies for reaching this group must be highly relational and clearly discovery-oriented. Such adults respond best to invitations that promise to build relationships with adults of similar ages. Social events, such as church or Sunday school class dinners, outings, cookouts, and recreational activities are just some of the approaches the successful soul-winner will use.

In such relationship-building experiences, we must work quite diligently to not press beyond the intimacy level they are comfortable with but, at the same time, also press beyond a superficial level. To find this level takes careful observation and sensitivity. You want to uncover true needs. You need to strip away superficial self-armor, but only as their tolerance for intimacy increases through increased relational contact.

These relational experiences should be structured so that those life experiences common to this age group are addressed, explored, and seen in the light of the Word of God. The goal is to build confidence in the relational group. The more this group is seen as one that is genuinely interested in them as people, not as statistics, the more the older adults will look to this group as the place where they can expect to find insight into truths that will give satisfactory answers to the life dilemmas they face.

Now, you may say, "where does the gospel come in here?" It comes in as positive foundations of trust are laid in the relationship bonds that are created and the confidence that we are pilgrims together in this life journey. When these factors are felt, there is an openness to the gospel. It is infinitely easier to accept that one is truly a sinner when one's trusted peers believe that. It is far easier to trust what the Word of God says about salvation when it is demonstrated that the Bible is contemporary and personal and trustworthy regarding life.

The statistical incidence of conversion in this age group is less than the earlier age groups. However, when these relational and life-discovery approaches become the thrust of the evangelism effort, the results are positive indeed. We are not saying that older adults are won to Christ by groups. The best evangelism is personal evangelism. However, to bring the older adult to the place of openness and receptivity to the gospel, building the proper relational bond and trust that the Bible is dependable regarding the issues of real life is essential. It is in this setting of fresh discovery and trust that older adults are most open to receiving Christ as their Lord and Savior.

Summary

The adult category covers a wide range of ages. With this range of ages comes a wide variety of interests, experiences, and needs. The three divisions of adulthood explored in this chapter—young adults, middle adults, and older adults—each have specific needs which come into play when sharing the gospel with them.

Young adults (18-24) are characterized by change and transition and are ripe for a commitment to Christ. Middle adults (25-50) are looking to establish long-term relationships which will provide stability for the future. What better long-term relationship to nurture than one with the Lord and Savior. Older adults (over 50) are at a point in their lives where they are fulfilling earlier goals. They are also interested in relationships and the focus of ministry to them must meet this need.

Evangelism to adults can be successful when, by concentrating on the needs and interests at the various stages of life, ministry is geared to meeting their needs.

Notes

1. Religious Education Association, "Faith Development and Your Ministry: Report Based on a Gallup Survey conducted for the REA of the US & Canada" (Princeton, NJ: The Princeton Religion Research Center, 1985).

Discussion questions

1. What characteristics of young adults make them ripe for the gospel?
2. What is the best evangelism strategy to use with young adults?
3. Describe the major characteristics of the middle adult.

4. How can the church best reach the Boomer age group?
5. What two aspects of older adulthood are most prominent?
6. Why can the church play an important role in the lives of older adults?

Application activities

1. Using one of the three groups discussed in the chapter, role play (for about three minutes) with a partner a typical situation that may face someone of this age group. Be sure to incorporate one or more of the characteristics and issues mentioned in the chapter.
2. Interview a young adult, middle adult, and older adult, asking the following questions:
   • What are the major choices you have to make in your life?
   • What has been the biggest adjustment during this stage of your life?
   • What types of things do you worry about when you worry or are concerned?

   From their answers try to identify issues addressed in this chapter.
3. Into which age group do most of your non-Christian contacts fit? Identify at least three characteristics of that age group and explain how understanding them will help you to better witness to these people.

TEAM EVANGELISM:
A PEOPLE-REACHING
STRATEGY

9

Team evangelism could also be called "Friendship Evangelism." It is an exciting outreach strategy which has stirred many churches to reach out with renewed zeal. Team evangelism is new only in the sense that it has not been organized as such until recently, but it is as old as Andrew bringing his brother Peter to Christ. Team evangelism is a tool churches are using to reach the unchurched by reaching those in the members' circles of concern or spheres of influence.

Team evangelism is everyone in the church working together in the evangelism ministry, each using their unique spiritual gifts, to bring friends, relatives, associates, and neighbors to Christ. The phrase, "Friendship Evangelism," describes a principle of reaching others for Christ and His church through natural relationships.

Team evangelism is a program designed to involve all people and all spiritual gifts in the evangelistic outreach of the local church. This program uses people where they are most effective. Some serve best as "evangelists" who present the gospel to unsaved in their homes. Others follow-up or disciple new converts into the church. Then there are "encouragers" with the gift of showing mercy. They·encourage and exhort others to be helpful, and they help them resolve their problems. The fourth and fifth groups are the "intercessors" and "helpers," who support the outreach program in prayer and by caring for details behind the scenes.

A data-driven, Bible-based strategy

The two foundational principles upon which team evangelism is based are expressed in "The Law of Three Hearings" and "The

Law of the Seven Touches." These two principles refer to the results of research into the successful evangelistic strategies of churches that are growing.

The Law of Three Hearings

Research shows that the visitors to the church do not decide to accept Christ or to join the church the first time they visit. People will usually attend a church 3.4 times before making a meaningful decision to become a Christian or to unite with the church. This does not mean that some are not saved the first time they visit a gospel-preaching church. The timing of a person's salvation is totally dependent on God, but is somewhat effected by the person's current receptivity to the gospel and responsiveness to the church. The figure 3.4 is a statistical average and implies that those who make a permanent decision for Christ usually attend church at least three times before accepting Him.

The Law of Seven Touches

It takes more than three hearings to get a permanent response to the gospel. The newly-saved must be networked into the church if they are to attend regularly and grow in their faith. Also, the unsaved should be followed up conscientiously to encourage them to continue to attend church. Research shows that people are more likely to return for the second and third visit if they are contacted seven times after their first visit. These contacts, or touches, can be initiated by the church through letters, phone calls, visits, or other contacts. These seven touches also include the times prospects see the church message in the classified directory, billboards, advertisements, flyers, or church newsletter. The obvious conclusion is that the church that contacts the most people the most times will probably see the greatest results. Evangelistic results, however, never depend entirely on one aspect, such as the number of contacts a church makes with a prospect or the number of hearings given to the gospel. But when all aspects of evangelism are followed, including the laws of the three hearings and the seven touches, the more opportunities a person will have to respond to the gospel.

Targeting receptive/responsive people

The ability to target receptive/responsive people is the first reason for the success of team evangelism. The ideal candidate for salvation is *receptive* to the evangelist and *responsive* to the gospel. When Jesus told the parable of the soil, only one part of the field was receptive to the seed. That was the place where the crop grew and a harvest was possible. Team evangelism makes an effort to determine the part of the field ready for harvest and then sends the evangelist to gather that harvest.

Why target receptive/responsive people?
The church should, of course, evangelize all of its "Jerusalem" by using as many means as possible. Because time is short and resources are limited, it should also invest its priority time reaching those who are receptive/responsive people. This follows the biblical example and, through discipleship, produces greater results. Jesus clearly taught that evangelistic efforts should reach all (Mark 16:15), but concentrate on those who are receptive and responsive (Matt. 10:14). This principle brought about the turning point in the apostle Paul's ministry (Acts 13:46).

If a pastor or volunteer evangelism ministry worker can make only five evangelistic visits during a period of time, it would seem wise that he/she place priority on visiting those who are most receptive and responsive. Why? Because concentrating on receptive/responsive people is trying to be as fruitful as possible for Christ and being a good steward of one's time and resources. Good stewardship demands that time be invested where it will be used the most wisely for the glory of God.

In light of this stewardship, Christians must establish priorities for evangelism. They must be interested in reaching all, but must also determine where their evangelistic efforts are likely to be most productive, and give that area the most attention. That does not mean that Christians can forget or ignore the rest of the world, but it does mean that they need to make the most of opportunities when they encounter receptive/responsive people.

Stair-stepping people to Christ

A second important principle of team evangelism is stair-stepping people to Christ. Stair-stepping is nothing more than a systematic and natural approach of bringing people to Christ. It allows the Christian to keep the ultimate objective in clear focus and see where the person is in the process of evangelism. The unique quality of stair-stepping is that it takes the guesswork out of evangelism and gives a means of assessing progress.

The entire church ministry team must be aware of the stair-stepping goal. They will come in contact with people on different steps. Their aim is to network people into the church and stair-step them to a meaningful decision for Christ. The more exposure the unsaved have to the gospel, the more they will be compelled to confront its truth.

The key to getting started is determining where the prospect is in relationship to God. The evangelist then knows what entry level to make in witnessing to the unchurched. Once a relationship has been made, the process of evangelism is a matter of stair-stepping the prospect toward faith in Christ.

Stair-stepping is a holistic approach to the task of evangelism or disciple-making. It includes all that is involved in reaching the unsaved where they are and bringing them to Christ. It is moving people through the process one step at a time. The following chart illustrates the entire process. The initial contact could be made with a person at any level. An unsaved person is not required to begin on the first step. Therefore, stair-stepping can begin or end with any of the various steps in the process.

STEPS TO CONVERSION

7. Repent/accept Christ.
6. I am willing to be saved.
5. I recognize I am reconciled to God through Christ.
4. I realize sin has alienated me from God.
3. I realize I am a sinner.
2. I know I am responsible to God.
1. I know there is a God.

Stair-stepping is both supernatural and natural. Many things contribute to a person's coming to Christ, such as the power of the gospel, the convicting work of the Holy Spirit, and the drawing of the Father. The power of God that brings salvation resides in the gospel, not in any human program or humanly-devised scheme (Rom. 1:16). Only the Holy Spirit can convict the sinner (John 16:8ff.), and every precaution must be taken to see that no conscious or unconscious attempt is made to replace spiritual conviction with psychological pressure or human manipulation. Regardless of human effort, only God can draw sinners to Himself (John 6:44).

At the same time, it is neither logical nor biblical to expect atheists on the first step to make a decision to repent and trust Jesus Christ without taking some intermediate steps in their understanding and acceptance of the person of God. Also, before people can exercise faith in Christ, they must understand the provision Christ has made for their redemption (Heb. 11:6).

In evangelism, the decision to trust Jesus Christ by faith is preceded by many other decisions. Some of those decisions may be subconscious, or they may come so early in life that the person has forgotten making them, but they must nevertheless be made. Unsaved people do not repent and trust Christ until they see their need and understand the gospel. Looking at the stair-stepping process, it is obvious that each step is dependent upon the one before it. Stair-stepping is a natural approach for effective evangelism.

Bonding people to the church

The third essential principle of team evangelism is *bonding*. The process of bonding newcomers to the church is commonly referred to as post-evangelism, but it is actually a part of the biblical and holistic processes of disciple-making. After a person comes to know Christ, it is imperative to get the new believer assimilated into the church. As mentioned in chapter one, evangelism is presenting Christ Jesus in the power of the Holy Spirit, so that people shall come to put their trust in God through Him, to accept Him as their Savior, and serve Him as their King in the fellowship of His church.

A comprehensive approach to evangelism requires that provision be made for new Christians' normal growth and development. This requires that new Christians become bonded to a local church. That is where they will be brought under the ministry of the Word of God that will result in spiritual growth (1 Pet. 2:2), victory over sin (Ps. 119:9-11), answered prayer (John 15:7), growth in character, and strengthened faith (Rom. 10:17). The local church is also where new Christians will be able to grow through fellowship with other Christians (Heb. 10:25).

Bonding is a biblical pattern. The first church, the one started on the Day of Pentecost, grew more rapidly than any church since that time, yet those early Christians were able to effectively bond people to the church. Their felt needs were met by the church (Acts 2:42). Those who were already members were willing and anxious to make room for the newcomers (Acts 2:47).

A bonding strategy that works – seven touches

The principle of "seven touches" is one that many congregations have found useful in bonding people to the church. The principle is one that allows for a comprehensive follow-up strategy. When visitors come to the church on a Sunday (usually the most common time for persons to make a first visit to a new church) and fill out a "Visitor Information Card," they should be immediately followed up.

The first contact

The first contact should happen later on Sunday. Someone should call the visitors thanking them for visiting the church and try to establish three things. First, there should be an offer to answer any questions the visitors may have about the church. Second, the "Friendship Packet" (information about the church) should be mentioned. Third, visitors should be told that someone will phone for an appointment to bring the packet to them.

The second contact

The next contact occurs in the next day or so. The pastor should write a letter thanking the person for attending and covering much of what would have been said during the phone call. This could be a standard computerized letter that goes out to visitors, but each letter should be personalized to the recipient.

The third contact
The church secretary, or some other appointed person, should call to set up an appointment for a visit. This phone contact should be made by Tuesday evening. When suggesting a time, give people an approximate amount of time that appointments usually last.

The fourth contact
The fourth contact is often in the form of a letter, written to the prospects confirming the times of the visits. (Even though some letters arrive after the visit because of postal delays, many churches have still found this to be an effective addition to the cumulative effect of follow-up.) The letter should express interest in being of service to the prospects and their families and assure them that they are welcome to visit the church services as often as they can.

The fifth contact
On Wednesday or Thursday evening, a representative from a church ministry the prospects are likely to be most interested in should visit them. This could be a class leader, a fellowship group director, or a member of a specific care group. The visitor should tell prospects about the church ministry he or she represents and explain a little about the other ministries of the church. The visitor should also spend time simply getting to know the prospects better and offering to answer any questions about the church. Often, prospects may be open to discussing spiritual needs with the visitor from the church. The visitor should try to be sensitive to the prospect's needs and should look for ways to initiate spiritual discussions. On some occasions, unsaved persons can even be led to Christ during this time.

The sixth contact
Hopefully, during the visit, the church representative was able to get a fairly clear idea of where prospects are spiritually in the stair-stepping process. For the sixth contact, the representative should immediately take the time to follow-up the visit with a letter. This letter should help clarify for the prospects the next spiritual step they should take. It should also express thanks for the visit and extend another invitation to return to church and to become involved in its ministries.

The seventh contact
An informal follow-up with a phone call on Saturday inviting prospects to church the next day provides the finishing touches to a week of following up receptive/responsive persons.
By the end of the week, the casual visitors have met several people from the church and recognize that the church is

interested in them. It is very likely that these prospects will return to the church, and even feel welcome and accepted the following week.

The seven touches detailed above comprise an evangelistic, bonding strategy that some churches have found to be effective. Because every church's situation and setting is different, your church will want to adopt, adapt, or modify this program to best fit your needs using only some of the steps listed above. Or, perhaps you could think of other "touches" that could replace or add to the follow-up steps found here.

Summary

The challenge of evangelism through church ministries is not only to win the lost, but to bond them to the church. The emphasis of your outreach should be directed toward people while they are receptive to the church and responsive to the gospel. Then, when these people visit your church, they should be followed up using church volunteers and personnel where they are gifted and reaching people when they are reachable.

Discussion questions

1. How would you describe "team evangelism"?
2. Why is the "law of three hearings" significant?
3. What does the "law of seven touches" accomplish?
4. What is meant by the expression, "stair-stepping a person to Christ?"
5. What is bonding?

Application activities

1. In light of your spiritual gift(s), where would you best fit into the team evangelism outreach strategy of your church?
2. List several unsaved friends you have witnessed to and measure their progress toward conversion on the stair-stepping chart in this chapter.
3. If an unsaved person visited your church this Sunday, what should be done within the next week?

LEADING PEOPLE
TO CHRIST
IN THEIR HOME

$$\boxed{10}$$

Jesus commissioned the church to make disciples (Matt. 28:19). Because many people are more likely to respond to Christ in their home rather than in a church or other setting, churches need a program of visitation which attempts to introduce people to Christ in their homes. While many people can be involved in this program, those who actually visit others at home and share the gospel are considered to be *evangelists*.

Who are evangelists?

The Bible refers to evangelists as individuals who God has given to the church to equip others for the work of ministry. (Eph. 4:11,12). Philip was an evangelist. He went about leading people to Christ and baptizing new believers (Acts 8:35-38). His specific calling was evangelism. Scripture makes it clear, however, that all are to be involved in the ministry of evangelism. Paul exhorted Timothy to do the work of an evangelist (2 Tim. 4:5). Elsewhere in Scripture believers are admonished to share their faith with the unsaved (1 Pet. 3:15; 2 Cor. 5:18-21).

In team evangelism, the term *evangelist* is applied to those who share the gospel with the unsaved and lead them to pray to receive Christ. Most often, people think of evangelists as paid, full-time workers who visit cities and hold evangelistic crusades. But, more commonly, evangelists are volunteers in the church who are involved in the church's visitation program.

The work of leading people to Christ is a combined effort of several people with various gifts. It is not limited to one individual with the gift of evangelism. "We are God's fellow (team) workers" (1 Cor. 3:9 NIV). Some plant, others water, but it is God who gives the increase (1 Cor. 3:6).

When team evangelism is functioning in a church, receptive/-responsive people are in direct contact with several Christians who have a variety of spiritual gifts. As they are stair-stepped toward Christ, a believer will be close to them who is uniquely gifted to meet their need at the moment.

Function of the evangelist

The evangelist primarily focuses on the last steps a person takes in becoming a Christian. Everyone in the church is responsible for making initial contacts, establishing redemptive relationships, and stair-stepping people toward salvation, but it is usually the evangelist in a church's outreach program who is involved in leading people through the final process to the point of decision and salvation.

The specific way evangelists carry out their work will vary from person to person. Each will use their unique personality and gifts that God has given in sharing the gospel. The evangelist, however, will use four enabling spiritual gifts (see chapter 2)—faith, discernment, wisdom, and knowledge—to carry out the work of evangelism.

The actual work of the evangelist is to present the gospel in such a way that the unsaved understand it and are able to respond to Christ. Evangelists need to answer questions and concerns non-believers have about the gospel and create a climate of receptivity and responsiveness.

Enabling gifts used by the evangelist

Among the gifts needed for the evangelist to be effective are the gifts of faith, discernment, knowledge, wisdom, and several of the serving gifts.

The gift of faith

The evangelist must be a person of faith. Faith is the God-given ability to undertake a task for God and to sustain unwavering confidence that God will accomplish the task in spite of all obstacles. Leading a person to Christ is beyond the scope of human wisdom and power (John 6:44). The evangelist needs faith because he or she is constantly engaged in spiritual warfare. (1 Pet. 5:8; 2 Cor. 4:4). Faith is the only means of access to the power (Heb. 11:6) and protection of God (Eph. 6:16).

The gift of discernment

Every Christian has been given some discernment and is responsible for discerning the spirits (1 John 4:1), but the enabling gift of discernment is the special ability to distinguish between truth and error. Those who possess this gift have an acute ability to distinguish between things that are raised up by God and false imitations.

Those with the gift of discernment are not easily taken in by the deceit of Satan because they can see through his mask of pretense. This is important because Satan is a master counterfeiter (2 Cor. 11:14,15). He possesses antichrists, false prophets, false teachers, false apostles, false sheep, and false spirits who are eager to do his will. He has sown his tares among the wheat of God. Discernment is needed to distinguish between the real and the counterfeit.

Those doing the work of evangelism will encounter some who profess to be Christians and some who truly believe they are saved. These people may speak the language and act the part, but within they are not truly regenerated. Evangelists need to be able to discern when a professing Christian may not actually be saved. They need discernment to penetrate an unbeliever's protective shell.

Discernment will also help evangelists determine where the unsaved person is in the stair-stepping process and help them determine what the next step is for that person.

The gift of knowledge
Those doing evangelism must have knowledge if they are going to be effective. This includes not only a knowledge of the plan of salvation, but also a knowledge of Scripture in general. They must have a general knowledge to speak to objections that might be raised when presenting the plan of salvation. Knowledge can also include insight into people and the culture they represent. Paul exercised the gift of knowledge on Mars Hill when he shared information gained through observation (Acts 17:23), applied principles of Scripture to the situation (Acts 17:24-27), and even made reference to a poet of the Athenian culture to reinforce his message in the minds of the listeners (Acts 17:28). His knowledge was gained through his formal education at the feet of Gamaliel (Acts 22:3) and was enhanced by the spiritual gift of knowledge (1 Cor. 12:8).

The gift of wisdom
The enabling gift of wisdom is the God-given ability to use knowledge correctly in the achievement of spiritual goals. Like the other enabling spiritual gifts, wisdom is available to all Christians (James 1:5; Eph. 1:17). The gift of wisdom is the applied insight that the evangelist will use when stair-stepping a person to a spiritual decision. Those with this gift are endowed with a special talent for integrating all the available knowledge and bringing it into focus on a problem or question.

The gift of wisdom will be helpful in countering the arguments and answering the questions of the unsaved. Every Christian should "be ready always to give an answer to every man that asketh you a reason of the hope that is in you" (1 Pet. 3:15).

Other serving gifts

In addition to the above enabling gifts, those who do evangelism will be most effective in leading people to Christ in their home if they possess the gift of prophecy, teaching, or exhortation (see chapter 2). This does not mean that those who have other gifts cannot do evangelism. All Christians have a responsibility to determine how their gifts can be most effectively used and become involved in the process of reaching the unsaved for Jesus Christ. According to contemporary surveys, approximately 86 percent of all believers come to Christ through the influence of a friend or relative. It is crucial, therefore, that all believers be involved in the ministry of evangelism.

The visitation program

A church visitation program is a helpful tool for conducting evangelism in the community. Some churches have an organized visitation night, while others visit on a less regimented schedule. Regardless of the nature of the program, certain underlying principles should govern any outreach into homes.

Who to visit

As mentioned earlier, evangelistic efforts should be centered on those who are receptive to the church and responsive to the gospel. Most often, the best people to visit are those who visited a church service the previous week. Others who may be contacted include those who send their children to a church ministry but do not themselves attend, social contacts of church members who have indicated an interest in spiritual things, unsaved persons who regularly attend various church ministries, and those who respond positively to a community survey indicating a willingness to discuss the church or gospel in their home.

When to visit

The best time to visit will vary in each community, but a Wednesday or Thursday evening works well for churches using the bonding strategy discussed in chapter 9. Research suggests that a person is most likely to return to a church if they are contacted by a person from the church within 48 hours of their initial visit. Because of this, some may want to visit Monday evening, but a contact may be made by phone to establish an appointment for a later time. Many people do not appreciate an unannounced visitor from the church. They will have more time to give to the visit if an appointment has been made.

How to visit

When visiting, those doing evangelism should remember that they represent the Lord and the church. The person being visited may evaluate both on the basis of the visitor's appearance and behavior. The purpose of the visit is to explain the gospel and give the non-believer a chance to repent and accept Christ.

When visiting, try to begin by establishing a point of contact. Thank the person for attending a church service and speak briefly about the church's ministry. Next, offer to assist the family through various church ministries. Invite them to ask any questions they may have about the church or as a result of the visit. Often this will open an opportunity to present the gospel. The visitor could explain that one of the reasons for the visit is to share the central message of the church with others. This should lead to a sharing of the gospel in a systematic way, and the opportunity for the individual to receive Christ (see chapter 5).

Extending the visit

Regardless of the response of the person(s) being visited, leave the home in such a way that other visitors from the church can return and find a receptive person. Invite them to church that weekend. If they have not received Christ as Savior, try to arrange a visit the following week to discuss the matter further. It is usually best to keep a visit short, but the visit can be extended through a follow-up letter thanking them for allowing you to visit, reviewing the nature of the visit, and suggesting the next step in the bonding process.

The visit can also be extended by leaving literature from the church with the family. The church should produce a brochure outlining and encouraging participation in various church ministries. Some churches include a summary presentation of the gospel in their brochure while others insert an appropriate tract. Churches may also wish to include in the brochure a brief history of the church, pictures of individuals or groups from the church, a church logo or slogan, a message from the pastor and an indication of the church's future plans.

Helpers and intercessors

An effective visitation program does not happen without those gifted in service who can help behind the scenes. Intercessors, who can support the ministry in prayer, must also play an active part. People who feel uncomfortable visiting in homes can take part by keeping records, arranging visits, compiling visitation reports, preparing meals for those involved in the visitation program, and caring for children while parents visit the prospects in their homes. Others can support the program with their prayers, perhaps even praying for individuals by name as they are being visited or visiting others.

Training evangelists

As the church grows, more people will need to be visited and more believers will be needed to visit the homes. Those involved in the visitation program should pray for laborers (Matt. 9:38) and look for those with spiritual gifts that would equip them for this phase of church outreach. In most cases, they should be trained by those experienced in sharing their faith prior to being incorporated into the program. This training should include the study of evangelism, an orientation to the doctrinal beliefs of the church, and a briefing on the various church ministries. This training could also include some involvement with the actual home visits. It is usually best to visit in pairs, with one person doing most of the talking. During the instruction, the evangelist in training could be the silent partner, carefully observing the more experienced partner share the gospel. Later, the trainee should be given a more active role as we learn best by doing.

Summary

The visitation program provides opportunities for many Christians to serve, but those displaying gifts in evangelism should especially be involved in this ministry exercising their gifts as they share Christ with people in their homes. Visitation may be viewed as the harvest phase of the church's outreach, because people will more often respond to Christ in their homes where the gospel can be clearly and personally presented. This program can only be effective when other church members and ministries are functioning in outreach helping to target receptive/responsive people.

Discussion questions

1. What is an evangelist?
2. What is the function of an evangelist?
3. Who are the best people to visit in a visitation program? How do you find these people?
4. What should take place in an evangelistic home visit?
5. How can evangelists be trained?

Application activities

1. In light of your spiritual gifts, determine where you would best fit into a visitation program. Discuss with others in the class ways you could become involved in this outreach ministry.
2. Outline the steps you should take to become more effective in the work of evangelism. Then, set up a plan that will help you take these steps.

DISCIPLING
A NEW BELIEVER
TO MATURITY

11

Evangelism does not end when a person receives Christ as Savior. An effort must also be made to bond that convert to the church and to provide for Christian nurture and growth. The process is called post-conversion or post-evangelism. Just as a baby needs special attention as it grows toward physical maturity, so babes in Christ need others to help them grow toward spiritual maturity. A new Christian may become discouraged and fail to live for Christ if someone does not offer to help the convert to grow spiritually. Jesus wants our fruit to remain (John 15:16) and discipling new believers to maturity is essential if that goal is to be achieved.

The goal of discipleship

Encouraging spiritual growth is the goal of discipleship. This process begins when a person trusts Christ as Savior (see chapter 5) and continues for an indefinite period of time. In a sense, discipleship is a lifelong process; we should always be growing in our relationship to Christ. But in the weeks and months following a person's decision to trust Christ as Savior, the process of discipleship is of utmost importance. During this time the principles of growth need to become a part of the new believer's lifestyle. If new believers can be equipped and encouraged to develop habits of Bible study, prayer, fellowship, worship, ministry, and stewardship, they will experience rapid spiritual growth initially and continue to grow for years to come.

Bible study

The Bible is God's revelation of Himself to mankind. God is the source of this revelation (Deut. 29:29). Christ, the Son of

God, is the Bible's central theme (John 5:39). The Holy Spirit is the divine author of Scripture (2 Pet. 1:20,21). God gave the Scriptures to show people their sin (Rom. 3:9-20), Christ (John 5:39), eternal life (1 John 5:13), wisdom (Ps. 19:7), victory (Eph. 6:16,17), and God's expectations for their lives (2 Tim. 3:16,17). No wonder Jesus and Moses were agreed that people should live "by every word that proceeds from the mouth of God" (Matt. 4:4; Deut. 8:3).

If new believers are to experience sustained spiritual growth, they must be impressed with the importance of Bible study and be taught how to make the Bible an integral part of their life. First, they need to get into the habit of regularly hearing the Scriptures (Rom. 10:17). Second, if they can read, they should be reading the Bible daily (Rev. 1:3). They need also to study the Scriptures for themselves in a systematic way (2 Tim. 2:15). Young Christians will also find committing key Scripture verses to memory will help them in their Christian life. (Ps. 119:9-11). Finally, new believers should be encouraged to meditate on the Word, allowing it to change even their thoughts (Josh. 1:8).

Prayer

New believers also need to be instructed in prayer. Jesus viewed prayer with such importance that He taught it to His disciples by example (Mark 1:35), by parable (Luke 18:1), by principle (Matt. 6:5-8), and by pattern (Matt. 6:9-13). The pattern or model prayer Jesus used in the Sermon on the Mount is still the best tool to teach new believers the essential principles of prayer. As Augustine observed, "When we pray rightly and properly, we ask for nothing else than what is contained in the Lord's Prayer."

Jesus' method in teaching His disciples about prayer suggests some practical ways new believers can be taught prayer. First, those discipling new believers need to pray with them. Second, they will want to share stories of how God has answered their prayers. Third, they should teach the principles of prayer from the Scriptures. Also, just as Jesus gave His disciples a pattern in prayer, disciplers should give new believers a similar pattern.

Fellowship and worship

Another key to new believers' spiritual growth involves teaching the importance of fellowship and worship. This includes bonding new believers to appropriate fellowship cells within the church. As one studies the pattern of church growth in the early church, there appears to be two levels of church life. The cell was the first level, which was the smaller group meeting together for fellowship (cf. Acts 4:32). The second was celebration (worship), which was a larger gathering of the cells in a group for some corporate activity (cf. Acts 5:14). This type of meeting also involved preaching, worship, and public testimony. New believers need to become involved in both the small and large group aspects of church life if they are to experience sustained growth. Cells provide the infrastructure needed in a church. Most people will be bonded to a cell group (i.e., a specific church ministry) in the church before they become bonded to the church as a whole. Despite this fact, corporate celebration must also have a place. The two are complimentary, not contradictory. What is learned in cells is expressed in celebration. What is gained in celebration should strengthen the cell experience. Traditionally, these two levels are the worship service and the Sunday school class. But recently cell groups have expanded to include ministries like small group Bible studies, caring circles, and neighborhood fellowships.

Ministry and stewardship
Also, new believers need to be taught their privileges and responsibilities in ministry and stewardship. Because God has gifted all Christians, new believers need to discover their gifts and begin to develop them for ministry to other Christians and to the unsaved. They, too, might become part of the team evangelism outreach of the church. They will experience stronger growth if they are also taught basic principles of stewardship which help them acknowledge Christ's authority over their resources.

Discipling new believers
A new movement emerging in the contemporary church is discipling new believers one-on-one and sometimes in classroom situations. These disciplers help new believers get established in the faith and grow toward spiritual maturity. They primarily are involved in building up the saints and equipping them for effective Christian service. They attempt to get new Christians bonded to the church and firmly established in the faith. They help new believers grow to maturity and productivity in Jesus Christ. All Christians have a responsibility to help others mature in the faith.

The equipping ministry
The title "equipper" refers not to a spiritual gift but rather to a ministry function of gifted individuals. Christ gave gifted individuals to the church "for the equipping of the saints for the work of ministry, for the edifying of the body of Christ" (Eph. 4:12 NIV).
An equipper is primarily concerned with helping new believers after they are saved. They are responsible for helping new converts understand what has taken place when they trusted Jesus Christ, the basic doctrines and functions of the church, the importance and significance of baptism, how to have personal

communion with God, the importance of church membership and attendance, and the principles of good stewardship. They should be active in the process of getting newcomers bonded to the church. Once a new convert has become a church member, it is the equipper's responsibility to help them discover their spiritual gifts and find their place in team evangelism. They help believers continue to grow in grace and knowledge and remain productive members of the body of Jesus Christ.

Every Christian is different in terms of personality, background, spiritual knowledge, felt needs, and spiritual gifts (1 Cor. 12:12-30). Because they have these differences, the specific way the equipper carries out this ministry will vary. Each equipper must work according to his/her own ability, yet within the parameters set down by the church.

The equipper's gifts
As with every ministry function in the church, those who equip others need to develop their enabling gifts of faith, knowledge, wisdom, and discernment to maximize their effectiveness in ministry. Faith is the ability to trust God. Knowledge is the ability to search the Scriptures, summarize truth, and arrange it systematically. Wisdom is the ability to correctly use that information to achieve a proper end. Discernment is an expression of spiritual insight to distinguish between truth and error. As each of these gifts is developed toward its potential, equippers will be more effective in ministry.

In addition to the enabling gifts, equippers could also have gifts of teaching, exhortation, and/or shepherding. These gifts are described in chapter 2. Developing these serving gifts will help those who equip others be more effective in ministry as they teach new believers, spend time helping them in their Christian life, and watch over them as a shepherd watches over the sheep.

Encouragers that minister
"Encouragers" are another group of people who need to be part of the discipling process. They are not evangelists or equippers, but believers who are people-oriented and meet a fellowship need in a new believer's life and others in the church.

The ministry of encouragement
Barnabas was an encourager in the New Testament church and earned the reputation of being a "Son of Encouragement" (Acts 4:36 NIV). He may have had the gift of showing mercy (Rom. 12:8), as he apparently was able to identify and sympathize with people in need. He took Paul under his wing when others in the church viewed him as suspect (Acts 9:27) and later ministered to John Mark when he and Paul parted ways (Acts 15:39).

The encourager might be thought of as a "lubricating agent" who keeps things running smoothly. As the gift implies, the encourager's primary function is that of encouragement and motivation. Encouragers are constantly ready to assist people who need help. Sometimes they encourage through communicating the Word to people at their point of need. At other times, they encourage much by their example, just as Gaius encouraged the aging apostle John (3 John 1-4).

The encourager's gifts

Like other ministering Christians in the church, encouragers also need to develop and exercise their enabling gifts. The gift of discernment will help them see spiritual needs and potential problems before others, and will give them time to provide encouragement even before potential discouragement has begun to invade a new believer's life. Although they are not teachers, encouragers still need enough knowledge to give their ministry a firm foundation. Wisdom will enable encouragers to determine what truth to apply to a particular need and how to best provide encouragement.

Encouragers could also benefit from the gifts of exhortation and mercy-showing. The exhorter is the one "called along side" to help people. In a very real sense, encouragers are this kind of people helper. Those with the gift of showing mercy tend to empathize well with people and communicate love easily. This, too, is an asset to those engaged in encouraging others.

As with the ministries of evangelism and equipping, the ministry of encouragement can be performed by every Christian who has received encouragement from God in times of trial (cf. 2 Cor. 1:3,4). Those gifted in this area should consider this ministry as their primary service for Christ, but not to the point of neglecting other important duties of the Christian life. Likewise, Christians who are not gifted encouragers should not neglect opportunities to encourage one another when they can.

Where to find discipleship materials

One challenge encountered in discipling new believers to maturity is finding suitable materials which meet the specific need of a particular ministry. Often church leaders have developed their own discipleship materials or used parts of various programs and tailored them to their own ministry. Although church leaders may wish to develop at least one discipleship lesson which acquaints new believers with their specific church ministries, a number of parachurch interdenominational organizations publish evangelical discipleship materials that have been used successfully.

Evangelical Training Association has provided leadership training materials for over sixty years. For those who are especially interested in using a classroom approach to discipleship, it has a course titled *Growing Toward Spiritual Maturity*. This is one of several courses available through ETA, Box 327, Wheaton, Illinois, 60189.

Campus Crusade for Christ has developed an extensive series of discipleship lessons known as the *Ten Basic Steps Toward Christian Maturity* and has also produced a number of "transferable concepts" booklets useful in a one-on-one discipleship program. These and other Crusade publications are available through their office at Arrowhead Springs, San Bernadino, California, 92403.

Church Growth Institute is producing a series of equipping materials which emphasize a team approach to ministry based on discovering and using one's spiritual gifts. They are located at Box 4404, Lynchburg, Virginia, 24502.

Master Life is an intensive discipleship program which emphasizes developing the spiritual life as it relates to involvement in both the church and home. Initial course materials in the Master Life program have been of high quality and new courses are still being developed. Master Life materials are available through their office at 127 Ninth Ave. N., Nashville, Tennessee, 37234.

For many years now, the Navigators have been recognized for their emphasis on quality discipleship programs and materials. In addition to their "Topical Memory System," NavPress (the publishing arm of that ministry) produces numerous books and Christian growth materials including a series of study guides prepared for discipleship purposes. The Navigators may be contacted at Box 6000, Colorado Springs, Colorado, 80934.

Most Sunday school curriculum publishers and denominational offices produce discipleship materials designed for churches who use their other materials. You may wish to contact your publisher or denominational headquarters to determine what is available.

Summary

The church has a responsibility to disciple new believers to maturity. They need to be taught how to grow spiritually through Bible study, prayer, fellowship, worship, ministry, and stewardship. Believers with special gifts that enable them to minister as equippers and encouragers will be especially valuable in this aspect of team evangelism. All Christians need to invest themselves in training new believers according to a plan using discipleship materials which will help new believers mature.

Discussion questions

1. What are some of the principles of spiritual growth a new believer needs to learn?
2. Who is best equipped to train new believers? Why?

3. Why is the ministry of the encourager so important?
4. How are people discipled through church ministries?
5. If you lead a friend to Christ, what can you do to insure that this new believer grows spiritually?
6. What gifts are needed to be effective as an equipper or encourager in the discipleship process?

Application activities

1. Secure copies of the discipleship material used by your church and other groups. Evaluate its possible usefulness to a new believer.
2. Identify someone in your sphere of influence that you could help to grow in Christ. Look for opportunities where you can help equip and encourage this person in his or her relationship with Christ.

PRAYER

IN

EVANGELISM

12

Prayer has been prominent throughout the history of the church. Great people of God have been great people of prayer. They knew the discipline of seeking after God in prayer. These people served God well. They were able to accomplish great acts of service to God because they were often on their knees.

Christians who attempt to share their faith without including prayer as a vital part of the process are making their task difficult, if not impossible. Lewis Chafer's book, *True Evangelism*, emphasizes the role prayer plays in evangelism. In it he says, "While the work of saving the lost must ever be a divine undertaking accomplished only through (Christ's) finished work on the cross, there are aspects of the work of seeking them which are committed to his followers ..."[1] Evangelism must not be done by human effort. Prayer is the bridge between divine sovereignty and man's initiative in leading people to Christ.

The spiritual poverty in much Christian educational work today simply has no excuse. The power for accomplishing a spiritual work is at the disposal of Christians. Paul, under the inspiration of the Holy Spirit, wrote "And pray in the Spirit on all occasions with all kinds of prayers and requests. With this in mind, be alert and always keep on praying for all the saints" (Eph. 6:18 NIV). The comprehensiveness of prayer is seen in the use of "always" and "all" throughout the verse. Prevailing prayer must be constant and persistent.

Importance of prayer

When we look into God's Word the importance of prayer in evangelism becomes clear. There we find that it was both commanded and exemplified by persons in the Bible.

Commanded

A quick survey of the Scriptures indicates numerous commands for Christians to pray. "Call unto me, and I will answer thee, and show thee great and mighty things, which thou knowest not" (Jer. 33:3). "Pray without ceasing" (1 Thess. 5:17). "Be careful for nothing; but in everything by prayer and supplication with thanksgiving let your requests be made known unto God" (Phil. 4:6). Prayer clearly has a basic place in God's program. It enables believers to unite with God's purposes. Through prayer church volunteers are dealing directly with God. Prayer is the channel through which they labor to win others to Christ.

Exemplified

Prayer is exemplified by many people throughout the Bible.

Old Testament reveals numerous examples of prayer supporters. Abraham, the friend of God, interceded in behalf of Lot. Joshua prayed for the sun and moon to stand still until God's people put their enemy to flight. Jacob was a man of prayer, who believed in the God of prayer. Moses was called a mighty intercessor. Often his prayer would offset the terrible stroke of God's wrath upon the rebellious nation of Israel. Elijah so stayed the course of nature through prayer that James exhorts Christians to pray as Elijah prayed (James 5:17). Prayer brought health to King Hezekiah. Great and widespread repentance happened among the people of Israel as the result of Ezra's prayer. He was the great mover in the great work for God. Nehemiah is another example of building through prayer. His prayer and the building of the walls of Jerusalem went side by side. Daniel was first and foremost a man of prayer. His prayer broke the plot of formidable politicians who lobbied against him. He prayed not only in time of crisis, but made prayer a daily practice. People in the Bible prevailed in God's work because they persistently and consistently persevered in prayer. The work of evangelism through volunteer church ministry can prevail today if leaders will pray.

Christ exemplified prayer. The gospels indicate that prayer is the foundation of the Lord's method in every undertaking. "The prayers of Jesus discover to us the wellspring of His wisdom and power, the soul of His method, and the root and recipe of all life lived under the smile and by the power of God."[2]

Jesus lived a life of prayer. Jesus should be our authority and example in prayer. Prayer was important to Him. Notice how He taught His disciples to pray. He took time to show them how to compose their prayer (Luke 11:2-4). In John, chapters 14 through 16, we are given the formula for prevailing prayer. Christians are exhorted to ask in Jesus' name. This does not mean we should merely affix His name to our prayers, but that it is only in the person of Jesus that we have access to the Father. He honors our requests because Christ is our basis of approach to God. The terms "pray" and "prayer" are used at least twenty-five times in connection with the Lord in the brief record of His life in the four gospels and His praying is mentioned in other places where the words are not used. The gospels record seventeen instances of prayers in His life. His earthly life reveals to us this dynamic for Christian service and witness.

The Lord spent time in prayer, "And in the morning, rising up a great while before day, he went out, and departed into a solitary place, and there prayed" (Mark 1:35). Also, he set aside a place for prayer, "And it came to pass in those days, that he went out into a mountain to pray" (Luke 6:12).

Paul was a man of prayer. Prayer was also the dynamic in Paul's life. Paul S. Rees writes, "If this man Paul was mighty and massive as a man of thought, and as a man of action, and as a man of vision, and as a man of eloquence, he was mighty and massive also as a man of prayer."[3] Paul's various epistles are filled with prayer. Prayers are written into the paragraphs of his letters (Eph. 1:16ff.; 3:14-21), and he frequently exhorts Christians to pray.

Values of prayer in evangelism

Prayer is the basis for a life-changing ministry. The history of the Christian church is a history of answered prayer. The first church in Jerusalem was born through prayer. The first converts in Europe were led to the Lord by Paul and his companions at the place of prayer (Acts 16).

When prayer is taken out of any Christian work, especially evangelism, the result will be the eventual failure of that work. Victories are won on the knees of God's servants.

Prepares the Christian for service

"Pray ye therefore..." (Luke 10:2) is not a request, but a command from the Lord. Prayer gives the Christian power and direction in ministry for Christ. Keeping in touch with God is the main assurance to Christian workers that their efforts will be pleasing to God.

Prayer causes self-inspection. Earnest praying will lead to refinement of the Christian's character, as it requires confessing and forsaking personal sins. It demands cleansing from the defilement of sin, thus bringing the believer into right relationship with God.

Prayer encourages confidence. Prayer helps Christians to be bold in witnessing for Christ. By prayer timid volunteers are given courage to teach and to tell of Christ. Bible-study leaders are given confidence to help others explore the Word of God. Christians in the workplace are given strength to be able to maintain integrity and share Christ with other workers. The early Christians prayed for boldness (Acts 4:29) and God answered. As a result, the ministry expanded. Prayer will give believers a ring of certainty, authority, and conviction in their ministry of evangelism.

Prayer sharpens understanding. Prayer gives teachers keen insight into their students' needs. It helps witnessing Christians understand those with whom they are sharing their faith. Because prayer causes believers to lean on God for the power for ministry, the Holy Spirit is then able to guide them in understanding and assessing each evangelistic situation and ministry experience.

Prayer clarifies methods. Prayer guides believers who are presenting the gospel in the approach to use and the words to use. Evangelism cannot be hurried; it takes time. Christians must invest time in prayer about their own personal Christian walks and their evangelistic ministries. When people withdraw in prayer, they can then help draw men to God.

Relates to the Holy Spirit

The effectiveness of prayer and the Holy Spirit's ministry are inseparably related in several ways.

Prayer releases spiritual power. Prayer enables believers to exercise their natural gifts in evangelism as energized by the power of the Holy Spirit. The best teaching materials or ministry abilities Christians possess are hampered by impoverished prayer lives. If anyone could have influenced people by sheer intellectual knowledge and natural gifts, Paul was that person. But even he urged Christians to pray for him that he might speak clearly.

Prayer unlocks the meaning of Scripture. Communicating the Word of God as a means to salvation is emphasized in the Bible (Rom. 1:16; Heb. 4:12; Rom. 10:14,15). Human instruments are needed to proclaim the gospel. But more than this, the Holy Spirit is the One who interprets the Scripture. Divine truth has no life-giving ministry apart from the Holy Spirit's life-giving energy.

Prayer prepares the unsaved. One of the gripping pictures of the unsaved is the analogy of blindness. Paul paints this picture rather vividly, "But if our gospel be hid, it is hid to them that are lost: In whom the god of this world hath blinded the minds of them which believe not" (2 Cor. 4:3,4).

Chafer writes that this "blinding or unveiling of the mind... causes a universal incapacity to comprehend the way of salvation, and is imposed by the arch-enemy of God in his attempts to hinder the purpose of God in redemption."[4] Sometimes this blindness causes men to think the gospel is foolishness (1 Cor. 1:18).

God's work of removing blindness includes convicting of sin and illuminating people's minds to see their sinful condition, to recognize Christ's death on the cross, and to seek God's forgiveness. This is the work of the Holy Spirit in answer to prevailing prayer.

Effectual prayer in evangelism

Prayerlessness can paralyze and short-circuit the church's effectiveness. Advertising, public relations, and promotional activities are poor substitutes because God's power for evangelism only comes through prayer.

The remarkable outpouring of God's Spirit is granted only to the church in which God's people "humble themselves, and pray, and seek (his) face" (2 Chron. 7:14).

God's power

Prayer declares our inability to do the work of God. We invoke His power, therefore, for our ministry of witnessing. God is looking for those who are willing to be partners with Him in bringing the lost to the knowledge of Jesus Christ.

Believers bear the name of Christ and are His representatives. They are privileged to use the name of Christ in their intercession. The name signifies the person. We come to God through the person of Jesus and have power with God.

Believer's spiritual condition

By virtue of their relationship to God, Christians are called to share the burden of evangelism through prayer. Certain conditions must be met for answered prayer. We are reminded, "God never mocks us by demanding impossible conditions."[5] If we meet His conditions, He will answer our prayer and people will be born again.

Disobedience is rebellion against God. It hinders the Holy Spirit's work through the volunteer church worker. Those who abide in Jesus (John 15:7) are promised answers to prayer, for prayer and obedience go hand-in-hand.

H. Clay Trumbull differentiated between faith in prayer and prayer in faith. He said, "Prayer in faith is a commanded duty; faith in prayer is not commanded, nor is it justifiable. Prayer in faith is always reverent and spiritual. Faith in prayer is too often superstitious and presuming..."[6] Therefore, Christians should not trust in their ability to pray, but should trust God who answers prayer.

Faith is more than intelligent belief and trust. It is an exercise of reaching out to God in faith, confident that He will hear and answer prayer. Often we limit God's answer to our prayers by our unbelief. Faith trusts God and receives from Him.

The Lord was displeased with the insincerity of the scribes and pharisees. He was able to discern beyond their words when he said, "This people draweth nigh unto me with their mouth, and honoureth me with their lips; but their heart is far from me" (Matt. 15:8). David prayed, "Thou desirest truth in the inward parts" (Ps. 51:6). God puts a premium upon a cleansed heart and life when we approach Him in prayer.

Expectancy is one of the conditions of prayer. An expectant person is an optimistic person. When one is eagerly awaiting God's answers to a petition, the atmosphere is electric and alive with hope. "What things soever ye desire, when ye pray, believe that ye receive them, and ye shall have them" (Mark 11:24). Those who are carrying out the work of evangelism must believe that God will save the lost and must go to Him with that expectancy.

Practical aspects of prayer in evangelism

In order to be effective in your prayer life as a church volunteer in the evangelism program, a number of essential aspects need to be kept in mind.

A time for prayer

Christians who wait for extra time for prayer will not find it. Life is usually too busy. It takes planning and effort to find time for prayer. Things that must be done are given place in daily timetables. Remember to schedule prayer time as well. When prayer times have been set aside and carefully guarded against intrusions, we are more likely to be regular and systematic in praying.

Do not hurry an interview with God. It may be fatal to prayer or lead to weak and feeble convictions and inadequate preparation for witness.

A place for prayer

Believers need a place for private intercession. The actual location is not important since those in Christ can enter into fellowship with God anywhere and anytime. But for a routine practice of prayer, having a regular place which will be free from disturbances is important. Here you can concentrate and labor in prayer for the unsaved.

A prayer list

Having a prayer list will avoid rambling in prayer. Prayer lists enable believers to pray intelligently for particular people and their specific needs. For teachers, the class list can be used as a prayer guide. Those involved in the church's outreach program can use a record of recent contacts for their list. Believers who are trying to share Christ at their workplace can make a list of the specific people to whom they would like to witness.

Continual prayer

A prayer that gets answers must be a continuing prayer (1 Thess. 5:17). We are not to faint or give up when we are praying for the salvation of our students, friends, family members, and co-workers. We are responsible to pray for them. "Ask, and it shall be given you; seek, and ye shall find; knock, and it shall be opened unto you" (Matt. 7:7). The language of the original text implies on-going prayer, telling us to keep on asking.

United prayer
It is not the amount of prayer, but the attitude behind prayer that brings answers. God must be delighted, however, to see people band together in prayer. "That if two of you shall agree on earth as touching any thing that they shall ask, it shall be done for them of my Father in heaven" (Matt. 18:19). Concerted prayer encourages others' faith.

Summary
Prayer is more than a way of opening a lesson, closing a Christian meeting, or beginning a meal. Prayer must have a more vital place in Christian volunteers' lives than a short time of intercession before a meeting. Believers must plead *for* souls before they plead *with* souls.

As prayer warriors, it would be well to bear in mind what Albert Simpson Reitz expressed in song:
Power in prayer, Lord, power in prayer
Here 'mid earth's sin and sorrow and care;
Men lost and dying, souls in despair;
O give me power, power in prayer!

Living in Thee, Lord, and Thou in me;
Constant abiding, this is my plea;
Grant me Thy power, boundless and free;
Power with men and power with Thee.

Notes
1. Lewis S. Chafer, *True Evangelism* (1901; reprint ed., Grand Rapids: Zondervan Publishing House, 1967), p. 3.
2. John Henry Strong, *Jesus the Man of Prayer* (Chicago: The Judson Press, 1945), p. 15.
3. Paul S. Rees, *Prayer and Life's Highest* (Grand Rapids: Wm. B. Eerdmans Publishing Co., 1956), p. 11.
4. Chafer, *True Evangelism*, p. 57.
5. Louise Harrison McGraw, *Does God Answer Prayer?* (Grand Rapids: Zondervan Publishing House, 1941), p. 165.
6. Henry Clay Trumbull, *Prayer: Its Nature and Scope* (Philadelphia: John D. Wattles & Co.), p. 53.

Discussion questions
1. Give scriptural examples of the importance of prayer.
2. In what ways does prayer prepare Christians for ministry?
3. Discuss how prayer relates to the Holy Spirit's work.
4. How does a believer's spiritual condition affect prayer?

5. What are some practical aspects that believers should consider when examining their prayer life? How have you seen these factors affect your own life?

Application activities

1. Inquire from several believers what part prayer had in their salvation. With others in the class, compare the answers of those interviewed.
2. Gather a group of believers in prayer for specific individuals. Invite each to pray for a person to whom he or she has been witnessing or desires to witness to.
3. Keep a prayer list, a prayer schedule, and a prayer record for one week. At the end of the week, evaluate your prayer activities.

Bibliography

Bertolini, Dewey M. *Back to the Heart of Youth Work*. Wheaton: Victor Books, 1989.

Brooks, Hal. *Follow-Up Evangelism*. Nashville: Broadman Press, 1972.

Chafer, Lewis Sperry. *True Evangelism*. 1919. Reprint. Grand Rapids: Zondervan Publishing House, 1967.

Coleman, Robert E. *The Master Plan of Evangelism*. Old Tappan, NJ: Fleming H. Revell Company, 1978.

Dausey, Gary. *The Youth Leader's Source Book*. Grand Rapids: Zondervan Publishing House, 1983.

Eims, Leroy. *The Lost Art of Disciple-Making*. Grand Rapids: Zondervan Publishing House, 1978.

Flynn, Leslie B. *19 Gifts of the Spirit*. Wheaton: Victor Books, 1976.

Gilbert, Larry. *Team Ministry: A Guide to Spiritual Gifts and Lay Involvement*. Lynchburg, VA: Church Growth Institute, 1987.

Graham, Billy. *How to be Born Again*. Waco, TX: Word Books, 1977.

Hadidian, Allen. *Discipleship: Helping Other Christians Grow*. Chicago: Moody Press, 1987.

Hendricks, Howard. *Say It With Love*. Wheaton: Victor Books, 1972.

Ingle, C., ed. *Children and Conversion*. Nashville: Broadman Press, 1975.

Ironside, Harry A. *Except Ye Repent*. Minneapolis: Bethany Fellowship, Inc., 1937.

Kennedy, D. J. *Evangelism Explosion*. Wheaton: Tyndale House, 1977.

Lewis, Larry L. *Organize to Evangelize*. Wheaton: Victor Books, 1980.

Lindsey, Hal. *The Liberation of Planet Earth*. Grand Rapids: Zondervan Publishing House, 1974.

Little, Paul. *How to Give Away Your Faith*. Downers Grove, IL: InterVarsity Press, 1966.

Little, Paul E. *Know What You Believe*. Wheaton: Victor Books, 1987.

McDowell, Josh. *Evidence That Demands a Verdict, Vol. I*. San Bernadino, CA: Here's Life Publishers, 1981.

McDowell, Josh, and Stewart, Don. *Answers to Tough Questions*. San Bernadino, CA: Here's Life Publishers, 1980.

McPhee, Arthur G. *Friendship Evangelism*. Grand Rapids: Zondervan Publishing House, 1979.

Miller, C. John. *Evangelism and Your Church*. Phillipsburg, NJ: Presbyterian and Reformed Pub. Co., 1980.

Richards, Lawrence O. *Youth Ministry*. Grand Rapids: Zondervan Publishing House, 1972.

Ridenour, Fritz. *Tell It Like It Is*. Glendale, CA: Regal Books, 1968.

Rinker, Rosalind. *You Can Witness With Confidence.* Grand Rapids: Zondervan Publishing House, 1962.

Ryle, J. C., *A New Birth.* Grand Rapids: Baker Book House, 1970.

Sanny, L. *The Art of Personal Witnessing.* Chicago: Moody Press, 1957.

Sisemore, J. *The Ministry of Visitation.* Nashville: Convention Press, 1960.

Soderholm, Marjorie. *Explaining Salvation to Children.* Minneapolis: Free Church Publications, 1979.

Towns, Elmer L. *154 steps to Revitalize Your Sunday School and Keep Your Church Growing.* Wheaton: Victor Books, 1988.

Towns, Elmer L. *Winning the Winnable: Friendship Evangelism.* Lynchburg, VA: Church Leadership Institute, 1986.

Trotman, Dawson. *Born to Reproduce.* Colorado Springs: NavPress, 1974.

Wagner, C. Peter. *Strategies for Church Growth.* Ventura, CA: Regal Books, 1987.

Zuck, Roy, and Benson, Warren. *Youth Education in the Church.* Chicago: Moody Press, 1978.